THE SHAAR PRESS

THE JUDAICA IMPRINT
FOR THOUGHTFUL PEOPLE

A doctor's prescription for financial security and success in learning

by Dr. Tuvia Meister

A SHAAR PRESS PUBLICATION

Published by **SHAAR PRESS**
Distributed by MESORAH PUBLICATIONS, LTD.
4401 Second Avenue / Brooklyn, New York 11232 / (718) 921-9000

Distributed in Israel by SIFRIATI / A. GITLER BOOKS
10 Hashomer Street / Bnei Brak 51361

Distributed in Europe by J. LEHMANN HEBREW BOOKSELLERS
20 Cambridge Terrace / Gateshead, Tyne and Wear / England NE8 1RP

Distributed in Australia and New Zealand by GOLDS BOOK & GIFT SHOP
36 William Street / Balaclava 3183, Vic., Australia

Distributed in South Africa by KOLLEL BOOKSHOP
Shop 8A Norwood Hypermarket / Norwood 2196 / Johannesburg, South Africa

ISBN: 1-57819-198-X Hard Cover
ISBN: 1-57819-199-8 Paperback

Printed in the United States of America by Noble Book Press Corp.
Custom bound by Sefercraft, Inc. / 4401 Second Avenue / Brooklyn, N.Y. 11232

*To my wife Rivka and
my five children*

*Elchonan Bunim
Moshe Eliezer
Chaim Mordechai
Shoshana Miriam
Shira Malka*

Rabbi CHAIM P. SCHEINBERG
Rosh Hayeshiva "TORAH-ORE"
and Morah Hora'ah of Kiryat Mattersdorf

הרב חיים פינחס שיינברג
ראש ישיבת "תורה-אור"
ומורה הוראה דקרית מטרסדורף

I am very inspired to see this new work written by Dr. Tuvia Meister.

This work shall serve to highlight the importance of using money to allow one to continue a serious commitment to limud haTorah.

Dr. Tuvia Meister is to be commended for his great service in providing a unique benefit to the Torah Community with his new book.

May Hashem allow him to continue learning Torah, becoming a greater Talmid Chochom, and inspiring others.

With Sincere Blessings and Best Wishes,

Rabbi Chaim Pinchas Scheinberg

רחוב פנים מאירות 2, ירושלים, ת. ד. 6979, טל. 371513-(02), ישראל.
2, Panim Meirot St., Jerusalem, P. O. B. 6979, Tel (02)-371513, Israel

RABBI MOSHE HEINEMANN
401 Yeshiva Lane
Baltimore, MD. 21208
Tel. (301) 484-9079

משה היינעמאן
אב״ד ק״ק אגודת ישראל
באלטימאר
טל. 764-7778 (301)

בס״ד

באתי בשורות אלו להביע התפעלות שלבי ברחותי ספרו של ידידי דר. טוביה
מייסטער נ״י שבו הוא מבאר שאיש מסודר יכול לגמור תנ״ך ומשניות שני התלמודים
מדרש רבה ותנחומא עוד עם ש״ס ו' חלקי שו״ע בעשרים שנה אם לומד רק שעה
אחת או שתי שעות ביום.

גם מבאר שאיש מסודר יכול לסדר ענינו ממון שלו באופן שבעת הצורך ממון
מעט נצרך ונעשה ממון הרבה.

ונשמע מזה האחריות שיש לכל אדם לסדר עניניו ע״פ דרך הטבע שאלם
יצטרך לתיתנת בשר ודם ולא לידי הלואתם שהרי כל יהודי נשוי אשה מחוייב
את עצמו בהכתובה לעבוד ולתמוך באשתו כפי ההלכה וגם צריך כהיות
רחמני על בניו ולפרנס אותם די ספוקם ברוחניות ובגשמיות.

סוף דבר הכל נשמע בספר הנ״ל מבאר המחבר היך איש מסודר יכול להגיע
לתורה עם קמח שאם אין קמח אין תורה ואם אין תורה וכו' ויישר טובו וחילו
לאורייתא.

ועז באתי עה״ח באחד בשבת לסדר והיה עקב תשמעון ארבעה עשר יום
לחדש מנחם אב שנת חמשת אלפים שבע מאות וחמשים ושבע לבריאת עולם
עשה בה״ר ברוך גד־ל־יה. כ־למשפחת היינעמאן החונף מתא באלטימארר

RABBI MOSHE HEINEMANN
401 Yeshiva Lane
Baltimore, MD. 21208
Tel. (301) 484-9079

בס״ד

משה היינעמאן
אב״ד ק״ק אגודת ישראל
באלטימאר
טל. 764-7778 (301)

With these lines I would like to express my feelings upon seeing the book by my friend Dr. Tuvia Meister נ״י. In his work, he explains that an organized person is able to finish *Tanach, Mishnah,* both Talmuds, *Midrash Rabbah, Midrash Tanchuma, Tur* with *Beis Yosef,* and the four sections of the *Shulchan Aruch* in twenty years if he learns just one or two hours a day.

He also explains that an organized person can arrange his financial affairs in a way that a little money can be blessed and become a lot of money.

Thus we can understand that it is vital for every person to plan his financial affairs according to the ways of the world, so that he should not need the gifts of others, nor their loans. For behold, each married Jew obligates himself with the Kesubah to work and support his wife according to the halachah. And he also must be merciful on his children and to adequately support them both spiritually and physically.

The author explains how an organized person can achieve Torah with sustenance, "for if there is no flour there is no Torah, and if there is no Torah [there is no flour]."

And to this I affix my signature, on the first day of *Parshas V'hayah Akeiv Tishm'une,* 14 Menachem Av 5757.

Moshe son of the *Chaver* Baruch Gedalya Heinemann
Baltimore.

free translation of Rabbi Heinemann's approbation

Dr. Meister rightly observes that the stock market doesn't go up "on doctor's orders," but his book is one of the best prescriptions for improving your personal financial situation that's appeared in a long time. His book is useful for the investment approach it discusses and indispensable for the financial lesson it teaches: a little money saved with discipline, invested conservatively, and allowed to grow can yield the freedom to created the life you want. Reduce your spending, invest what you don't spend in growth, let time and compound returns work for you — if Dr. Meister's patients, congregation, and readers take that lesson to heart, they will profit by the results.

—Donald R. Nichols
Author of Starting Small, Investing Smart

Individual investors do tend to panic during market turbulence. They often buy at the "top of the market" and sell at the worst time. Most people know the old adage, buy low and sell high, but few have the stomach to do this. While it is true that equities outperform fixed-income investments in the long haul, you have to remember that risk is inversely correlated with return. If you invest in a passbook account, you will earn a low but sure rate of interest. Stocks have a much higher expected return but much more volatility and no guarantees. There is no investment that will pay a high return without risk. Different people have different degrees of risk tolerance. You have to know yourself.

In general, though, Dr. Tuvia Meister brings to light some of the tried and true principles of long-term investing, in particular "dollar cost averaging," putting away a fixed amount of money at regular uninterrupted intervals over long periods of time. The method works in such a way that your regular contribution automatically buys fewer shares at higher prices and more shares at lower prices. Through the power of compounding, your money will grow exponentially in the later years, especially if you have the discipline to start at an early age. Dividend reinvestment in additional shares increases the compounding effect. Dollar cost averaging is safer than "timing" the market by investing or withdrawing large sums all at once.

A portfolio of diversified stocks would include different industries: utilities, retail, financials, technology, manufacturing, and other. In general, it is best to avoid stocks which do not pay a dividend, do not have a long enough track record, or are involved in technologies or businesses you do not understand. It is also important to know that an excellent company can be an unattractive investment if its stock price is inflated relative to its value based upon future earnings. Over time, however, the price of the stock will come back into line.

Younger people should be more heavily weighted in equities. The percentage allocated to bonds and money market securities should be increased as people approach and then enter into retirement. One popular but somewhat arbitrary formula is to subtract your age from 100; the resulting number is the percentage of your savings you should allocate to stocks.

Don't underrate the importance of budgeting. The surprise best seller of the year, *The Millionaire Next Door*, supports Dr. Meister's discussion of frugal living and the importance of living off less than one's income. Those luxury homes and automobiles often belong to people the book refers to as Under Accumulators of Wealth, those with good incomes but large debt loads and inadequate savings. Conversely, Prodigious Accumulators of Wealth avoid hyper-consumption and are less concerned with status and image.

Patience, discipline, and calm have worked in the past. Investors saw paltry growth in the 1970s, but things sure have changed. So don't get discouraged. Make a plan and stick to it!

— Mr. Nathan Sax
Vice President, Mercantile Safe Deposit and Trust Company.

The Munk Group
36-35 Bell Boulevard
Bayside, NY 11691

718-281-7770
(Toll Free) 888-249-9150
(Direct line from Israel) 177-150-1817

February 10, 1998

During our 38 years of experience in investing, we have seen many people think that quick profits can be made in risky and speculative investments. We assure you this is not so. It is encouraging to see Dr. Tuvia Meister, someone outside the financial arena, publish a book targeted to the "Yeshivish" community specifically related to this subject.

In the area of investments, or finance for that matter, many studies have proven that the best long-term approach to consistently making money and "beating the market" was found to be long-term conservative buy/hold strategies. Many very wealthy people who have repeatedly beaten the market with very simple approaches have documented and re-documented their strategies. Famous names such as Benjamin Graham, Warren Buffet and Peter Lynch, to name a few, have been telling their tale in numerous books and articles of simple ways to make money in the market, but few take heed.

Literally, thousands have analyzed this phenomenon and we'll sum it up in two short reasons. First it takes "patience" and second, "discipline." Yet, we find that many people do not make money in the market - why is this so? It is because they lack patience and discipline - and realism as well. These are the people who should read this book.

In "The Meister Plan: A doctor's prescription for financial security and success in learning", Dr. Meister presents these steps in a very thought-out, easy approach. We applaud all of Dr. Meister's work in showing that what is thought to be a very complicated and confusing topic, is truly straightforward and realistic. If you follow Dr. Meister's steps, we believe one can reap the rewards the stock market has to offer, and in the long run achieve financial security.

Judah Munk

Nathan Munk

Aaron Munk, CFP

Contents

FOREWORD 10

ACKNOWLEDGMENTS 15

PREFACE — WHY A FRUM INVESTING GUIDE? 18

A WORD OF CAUTION 27

INTRODUCTION — A HOT NEW FUND 32

CHAPTER 1 — GOING HOME 35

CHAPTER 2 — BEING HOME 52

CHAPTER 3 — POOR PHYSICIAN 56
It's not what you earn that counts, it's what you save

CHAPTER 4 — BUDGETING TIME FOR TORAH 61

CHAPTER 5 — STOCKS VS. THE STOCK MARKET ... 79
It's not a stock market, it's a market of individual stocks

**CHAPTER 6 — MORE THOUGHTS ON STOCK
MARKET RISK** 84

**CHAPTER 7 — INDIVIDUAL STOCKS VS.
MUTUAL FUNDS** 88
I have beaten most funds and so can you

CHAPTER 8 — DIVIDENDS 95
*The single most important factor for long term
investment success*

**CHAPTER 9 — SIMPLE TOOLS OF FUNDAMENTAL
STOCK ANALYSIS** 111
*How I picked my 22 stocks. With the proper information,
stock selection can be easy and low risk*

CHAPTER 10 — THE MEISTER FUND   124
How the right combination of stocks can sizzle more than the individual parts

CHAPTER 11 — THE STORIES   128
My 22 stocks in a nutshell

CHAPTER 12 — THE REST OF THE STORIES   133
Extensive detail on all 22 stocks, with emphasis on dividend information

ABBOTT LABS	138
AMERICAN WATER WORKS	142
BOEING	145
BRISTOL-MYERS SQUIBB	148
CINCINNATI BELL	152
COCA-COLA	156
CONSOLIDATED NATURAL GAS	161
DOVER CORP.	164
DUKE POWER	168
GENERAL ELECTRIC	170
GILLETTE	175
HEINZ	177
HEWLETT PACKARD	181
LILLY DRUG	183
MERCK	186
MICROSOFT-INTEL	189
3M / MINNESOTA MINING AND MANUFACTURING	191
PNC BANKCORP	195
TECO ENERGY	199
WACHOVIA BANKCORP	203
WISCONSIN ENERGY	206

CONCLUDING THOUGHTS   211

APPENDIX I — SUGGESTED READING LIST   212

APPENDIX II — GETTING STARTED   215

Direct-buy and dividend-reinvestment programs

APPENDIX III — RECOMMENDED INDEX MUTUAL FUNDS   220

APPENDIX IV — SAMPLE INVESTING PROGRAMS   222

APPENDIX V — CUSTOMIZING THE PLAN   224

Suggestions on purchasing the stocks which I have described in this book

APPENDIX VI — PLEASE, TAKE NOTE   229

How to remember and access your learning

FOREWARD

by: Rabbi Mordechai Shuchatowitz
Rabbi, Agudath Israel of Greenspring, Baltimore, Md.

There is something very special, even inspirational, about the approach evident in the planning described so interestingly in this book. It deserves to be brought out and clarified, so that it can be fully appreciated. I hope I can express it adequately, בעזה"ש.

Firstly, on the financial level, let's assume that the plan itself has merit, which I make no pretensions of being capable of assessing, but which others more expert than myself seem to concur with, and which Dr. Meister's own years of experience seem to bear out. If so, it may prove to be an invaluable asset, providing much needed guidance to many of our families that struggle so terribly with making ends meet on a day-to-day basis, and have little or no reserves to provide for special expenses, such as weddings and other occasions, let alone early retirement. All too often, we hear of families practically facing financial destruction, fallen into a hopeless heap of debt, unable to find any way out other than accepting charity, the last thing they'd ever want to do. All is in G-d's hands, הכל בידי שמים, and this may be an unavoidable part of His Master Plan, but if we can do something to help avoid such disaster, we certainly should try. If this program can help even one family avoid such disaster by managing its money more effectively and efficiently, it's already worthwhile.

Together with its ambitiousness, this plan incorporates integrity too. It is completely on the level, Halachically as well as legally. This is not a "get-rich-quick" scheme that stretches the limits of the law and of Halachah, not a "pyramid" scheme that attempts to enrich some at the expense of other. Rather, these are perfectly legitimate investments in businesses through which the investor fairly shares their profits. It's like putting corporate America to work for you! After 120 years, when put to the test of the ultimate questions, I think one will be fully able to give an affirmative answer to the question: נשאת ונתאת באמונה," Were you trustworthy in your business dealings?"

An additional advantage that ought to be pointed out on the financial level is that this plan is noncompetitive, not limiting the room for others to do the same, to benefit similarly from Dr. Meister's research and experience. There is as much opportunity for others to follow his example, even if they copy his investments exactly, as there is stock available on the market. To the contrary, the more the better. Everyone benefits from the spread of this knowledge and from additional followers.

This is a welcome alternative to business opportunities that depend on secrecy, being shared only with a select few "insiders," purposely leaving the rest out, to somewhat selfishly safeguard the profitability of the opportunity, reserving it for only the chosen few. Somehow, the Torah's emphasis on חסד, kindness, on ואהבת לרעך כמוך, loving others as one's self, and on אמונה ובטחון faith and trust, don't seem to encourage such competitive approaches. The Chazon Ish writes beautifully about how an ehrliche Yid, a religious Jew, should actually **help** his competition, and realize that his own success will not be hurt by theirs. Amazing, isn't it? Not exactly what they teach in the MBA programs. This can be a constant challenge for many in business, and is in direct conflict with many profit-making schemes. But "The Meister Plan" avoids such problems, and is entirely consistent with these perspectives, inviting others to come and join and reap the benefits equally.

But on a deeper level, I am more impressed with the conceptual approach behind the plan. The very idea of long-term planning, of taking a serious look at the big picture of one's life ambitions and deciding how to get there, is something special, something that deserves our attention. It comes as a welcome break from the hectic pace at which we commonly run through life, a breath of fresh air, fragrant with purpose, with long-term vision, rather than with short-sighted hand-to-mouth satisfaction of pressing needs, reacting only to the immediate and the momentary. The haphazardness that today's over-busy lifestyle engenders, almost demands, so often precludes any long-range planning. We can hardly handle the pressures of the moment—how can we worry about providing for tomorrow?

You present a totally different model of life, one carefully planned in advance, thought out with a presence of mind, with a conscious purpose and direction. You choose the path you want to travel before you start out, rather than after you're stuck in a situation that you can no longer control. This is an exercise of your free choices, rather than being pushed along by others and running along in a "rat-race" pattern. It's living with a חשבון, *calculation*, figuring out where you're going, charting the path you wish to travel, taking the controls in your hands and maintaining your ship's direction, rather than letting it cruise along in "autopilot," almost aimlessly, until it may crash. This sense of planning in leading one's life is a very significant element in many aspects of living a Torah-true life.

The *Mesillas Yesharim* repeatedly decries the effects of the hectic pace that so inhibits our ability to concentrate on long-term goals. His opening line emphasizes the crucial place that such direction occupies in true service of Hashem. In the fifth chapter he lists being too busy as the first obstacle to the critical trait of caution, precluding our ability to pay attention to what we're doing. He aptly describes such a situation as having one's mental faculties tied up in the chains of one's preoccupations. Later, in Chapter 21, when explaining the means through which the lofty level of *chassidus* is attained, he states that even one who has reached this high spiritual level could easily lose it by being overly busy. We can see how significant a role overcoming this challenge plays in our life's work.

Ramchal, in the second chapter of *Mesillas Yesharim,* finds a source for this concept in Pharaoh's response to Moses' mission. He ordered his taskmasters to increase the workload of the Jewish people so that they would be too busy to pay attention to Moses. Pharaoh's intent was to preoccupy us with busywork for the purpose of restricting our ability to consider our position, and to make any meaningful plans. The physical enslavement was specifically designed so as to enslave the mind and the spirit. Furthermore, *Ramchal* attributes the same psychology to our archadversary, the *Yetzer Hara*, who attempts to prevent us from thinking carefully about what we are doing in our lives, by keeping us constantly preoccupied with diversions that fill our time and minds. It seems that the present-day evil inclination has chosen to redouble his efforts in this area, following the strategy outlined in the *Mesillas Yesharim* to an extreme.

The same long term planning and organization is evident in Dr. Meister's learning program as well. I'm glad to see that he has included some description of it in the book. I am already personally familiar with his systematic approach to mastering Torah learning, as well as with his continuous series of *siyumim*. Starting from the most elementary beginning levels and gradually progressing, step by step, up a ladder of skill building and knowledge gathering, he has developed a most impressive familiarity with the entire body of Torah learning, with an all-inclusive breadth.

But planning is only part of his formula for achievement. Discipline, sticking to his chosen plan, is the other. All the choices and plans would never get him to his goal if he could not remain on course for the full term of the voyage. Sure, a 25-year learning program sounds great, but it wouldn't amount to much more than good intentions, if one isn't able to keep a steady eye on the objective, and continue ever onward, step by step, until achieving the goal, reaching the chosen destination. The same is true on the financial front. As good as an investment plan may be, if one couldn't maintain the self-control to allow it to mature, to ride the temporary bumps and falls of the market without impulsively withdrawing funds, ditching ships before arriving at the aspired goal, the plan will not work. It takes a clear-sighted strength and resolve to resist the temptations of opportunities for instant gain, keeping in mind the commitment to the long-term goals one has set for himself. Planning and perseverance, decision and discipline, are the critical elements that combine to yield such accomplishments.

Unfortunately, both of these qualities seem to be rare commodities these days. Not only does the frenzied pace of contemporary life make it difficult to plan more than a few steps ahead of ourselves, it also often prevents us from carrying through on even small commitments that we occasionally make. How many times have we undertaken to learn some Mishnah by the end of a 30-day mourning period, only to cram most of it on the last day or two? Such a minor goal, such a short term. So attainable, yet so elusive. It's really frustrating, even depressing. It's all the result of too busy a life style. Not enough time to think carefully about what we're doing, let alone to do what we know we should. Pharaoh had it right— keep people too busy to think.

The model in this book, on the other hand, is almost reminiscent of the great *baalei mussar* of old who gradually and steadily developed themselves throughout the course of their lifetimes, working first on one trait and then on another, constantly honing, sharpening, improving and strengthening their own characters, ever striving to reach the perfection they demanded of themselves.

This is why I find "The Meister Plan" so inspirational. It is a "shot in the arm," invigorating, and encouraging, a beautiful model of what we can accomplish with careful planning and with disciplined adherence to our plans, both spiritually and materially. I consider it an act of generosity that Dr. Meister is sharing this work with the public in published form, so as to allow many others to gain from his example. All together, this is a major accomplishment that should bring his and his dear family, and thousands of readers, much joy and satisfaction, בעזה"ש.

Acknowledgments

open with overwhelming feelings of gratitude to Hashem for granting me the privilege of becoming *frum* and allowing me to learn Torah. With appreciation and honor I acknowledge an unpayable debt to my parents, Mr. and Mrs. Joseph Meister of Jackson Heights, Queens. They raised me to value family and education, always stressing that financial resources are a means to achieve proper spiritual goals, but not a goal in and of itself. Thanks to my in-laws, Dr. and Mrs. David Lowitz of Richmond, Virginia, who in returning to their Jewish roots imbued my wife Rivka with the same ideals. May our parents have *nachas* from all of their children and grandchildren.

Special thanks to the small, warm, wonderful Jewish community in Albany, New York who welcomed me when I became *frum* many years ago. Thanks to the Steins, Younkers, Langers, Mogilenskys, Blinders, Luchins and so many other families who took myself and other students into their hearts and homes week after week, year after year. Dr. Yirmiyahu Luchins, originally from Albany, provided me with my first taste that Torah learning is more important than secular professional pursuits. It was in his living room in Washington Heights that I was first overwhelmed with awe upon viewing his large majestic maroon-bound volumes of *Mishnah, Shas, Rambam, Tur* and *Shulchan Aruch* from which he was learning. I was filled with the feeling that these books with their rich yellowed pages contained true wisdom. The desire to try and learn what those volumes contained continues to burn within me from that day over 20 years ago.

Thank you to all of my *rebbeim*, study partners, and friends over the years at Yeshivah Sh'or Yoshuv, Yeshivah Ohr Somayach, and Yeshivah Kol Yaakov. Special thanks to Rabbi Leib Tropper, my *Rosh Yeshivah* from Kol Yaakov in Monsey, who has guided me through 20 years of life and learning. He has always made himself available in times of need for questions and guidance, always showing the warmth and concern of a true *rebbi* to his *talmidim*. Rabbi Tropper first brought my manuscript to the attention of his *Rosh Yeshivah*, Rabbi Chaim Pinchas Scheinberg in Jerusalem, who endorsed the idea that members of the Torah community could regularly invest small amounts in conservative stocks as a means of providing for the future.

Rabbi Scheinberg graced our home with a visit last year. Our entire family still feels the holiness left by his presence. We tremble at the memories of having the *Rosh Yeshivah* speak to us and bless us.

Ilana Meister is aware of her contribution but her modesty limits me to a simple thank-you.

Thanks to my friend Mordechai Silverman for his foresight. He spied a rough manuscript of investing advice which I had written and encouraged me to expand on it and adapt it for the observant community. Thanks for his early editorial assistance.

Thanks to my neighbor Reb Shimon Apisdorf who exemplifies all that is good about the Torah way of life. Even though he runs a competing publishing company, he assisted me in many ways to prepare my manuscript for submission to Shaar. He did not see competition, he only saw the opportunity to help another Jew.

My deepest gratitude to the editorial and production staff at Shaar Press. Their interest in this work and their attention to the many details involved is truly appreciated. I pray that my book fulfills their wish that it help families in our community to better prepare for their own and their children's futures in a safe, patient fashion.

My final debt of gratitude goes to my wife, Rivka Fruma. I tell her almost daily, and now I tell the world, that I would not be able to accomplish anything in my spiritual and learning endeavors without her help. She is unique among women, willingly forgoing the physical luxuries a physician could provide his wife, and instead desiring the spiritual benefits a *kollel* man can provide for his wife. May the Almighty bless us with long life together and may He bless us that we should see the fruit of our return to Torah Judaism by having good-hearted children, grandchildren, and future generations who are faithful to and learn Torah, do *mitzvos*, and perform acts of *chesed*.

Dr. Tuvia Meister
Shevat 5758

THE JEWISH WEATHER MAN

PREFACE

The cartoon is funny, but true. Observant Jews always qualify expressions about their future hopes and dreams with a prayer that it meets Hashem's will. I am not a weatherman. I am a physician with specialty training in pediatrics and diagnostic radiology, but today I learn Torah. Last year I retired from full-time medical practice at age 40 to pursue my Torah studies. I became observant while in medical school, over 20 years ago. Since that time I have tried to learn as much Torah as possible while working as a physician. But learning how to read Hebrew and studying Torah from scratch while attending medical school and practicing medicine was not easy to do. For many years I had nurtured a dream of retiring at the spiritually significant age of 40 to pursue full-time learning. Recently, I was able to do just that. This is a blessing from Hashem which is beyond my merits to deserve and which I appreciate with infinite gratitude.

Practically speaking, I was able to leave full-time work at age 40 because of years of conservative, patient investing. I carefully selected 22 conservative stocks, put them away, and allowed the dividends to automatically reinvest. I thought that the fundamental techniques of stock selection which I used would be of value to other observant Jews who have their own long-term goals such as making *aliyah* (emigration to Israel), learning in *kollel* (post-graduate Talmud study for married ment), supporting a child in *kollel,* or paying yeshivah tuition obligations. Having never come across an investment guide geared for this audience, I decided to write one. At first I was hesitant to pursue such a work because of the *hashkafah* (Orthodox philosophy) represented in the weatherman cartoon above. It would be difficult to write an investment book if every statement about market growth, stock appreciation, or profit increase was prefaced with the necessary myriad qualifications indicating that everything is in Hashem's hands.

For a non-Jewish audience I could write: "General Electric is a phenomenal company with excellent prospects for increasing profits and continually rising dividends." But an observant Jew knows that Hashem could bankrupt GE tomorrow if He saw fit. An observant Jew knows that 100 years of historical data on a company means nothing if Hashem plans something different for the future. Likewise, I only invest in companies that to my limited knowledge are ethical and productive members of society. But I cannot possibly know the true internal machinations of a multibillion-dollar organization with hundreds of thousands of employees. For the non-Jew I could write: "Hewlett Packard is a good corporate citizen and its founders were good American citizens." But I have no idea what the company and the founders are really like in the eyes of heaven.

Also, there are observant Jews who do not believe in various insurance products, financial planning, etc. Rabbi Shimon bar Yochai was able to live in a cave and have sustenance provided by Hashem. The Talmud says that if someone has enough bread for today, then thinking about tomorrow borders on heresy. This is one extreme of the attitude toward personal finance. It's proper and it's admirable, but it is also difficult for many of us to attain. On the other hand, to be overly involved with finance and investing — constantly monitoring the stock market, trading in and out while neglecting your Torah learning — is another extreme. This second extreme is certainly not the Torah ideal. My approach, as taught in this book, represents the middle ground. Expend some *hishtadlus* (effort) to select the stocks of some good companies and then take a hands off, long-term approach. The Talmud (*Bava Metzia* 42a) says that a person should put $^1/_3$ of his money in cash, $^1/_3$ in real estate, and $^1/_3$ in business. Equity stock investment in various companies can count as the $^1/_3$ to be put into business.

I have concluded that an investment book could be and should be written for observant Jews. There is a vast field of medical knowledge and physicians are taught that the human body works a certain way. An observant physician learns this information and accepts it. Yet he still says a prayer each day for *hatzlachah* in *refuah* (success in healing). A mother may know that a certain antibiotic always works for ear infections, but she still says a prayer when she gives the medicine to her child. Engineering, architecture, computer science, and many areas of professional endeavor all rely on accepted, established knowledge and all have their own set way of doing things. The observant professional follows the rules of his field, but in the end he knows that the patient is cured , the bridge doesn't fall, and the computer chip works because that is Hashem's will.

The investment field is no different. To the uninitiated individual the stock market may seem like a wild, irrational place, without rhyme or reason. If a person buys stocks based on hot tips from friends, without fundamental research of the company's financial history or present balance sheet, then the results probably will be wild and irrational. If a person concentrates daily on the constant ups and downs of the market, and continually trades in and out, he too will be in for a wild ride. However, if a person rationally analyzes a company's past history and present financial state of affairs and then carefully and patiently invests for the long term, the stock market becomes a very rational and often very rewarding place to be.

Years ago I had to do some part-time radiology work in Dover, Delaware, which forced me to spend several days a week away from my family. At times I found it hard to concentrate on my Torah study while away from home, so I would spend a few hours each week studying the fundamentals of stock analysis and analyzing specific companies in the Dover Public Library. I then selected 22 stocks which had strong histories and which met the specific criteria explained in this book. Did it take a lot of time? Not particularly. If you use this book it should take you even less time than it took me. Does it take a lot of time today to keep up with my portfolio? I spend about five minutes a day checking up on things. Even that is only to give myself a relaxing break. My portfolio would do just fine without the five minute checkup. This is a hands-off long-term portfolio of stocks. For a time I lived in the Shomron in the settlement of Emanuel, near Shechem. This is about as far away from a broker and the *Wall Street Journal* as you can get. I have purposely picked stocks that can be safely ignored for long periods of time, even decades if need be.

Does it take a lot of money? It takes as little or as much as you can spare for long-term investing. Many companies allow you to buy small amounts of stock directly from them without brokerage commissions.[1] Once you buy a single share, usually for less than $100, you can then add monthly amounts of as little as $10. Dividends reinvest for free as well, even when they only amount to pennies. Whatever a person can safely spare for long-term investing will virtually certainly (*im yirtzeh Hashem*) increase at a far better rate long term in the stock market than in the bank. In *II Kings*, Chapter 4 we learn that Elisha visits a Shunammite woman. Our sages say that she was the wife of Ovadiah the prophet. She tells Elisha that there is

---

1. See II for a listing of companies which allow you to buy shares cheaply and directly from them.

nothing in her house except a jug of oil. Elisha performs a miracle and the small amount of oil in the original jug, which was only enough to anoint one small finger, increases and increases, overflowing the original jug and filling multiple other vessels. The commentaries explain that Hashem's blessing can only rest on something which already exists, even if it is but a minute quantity of oil. But the miracle could not be performed using a completely empty jar. A Jew must have at least a little something put away if Hashem is to make it grow. We are also taught that we must make some effort on our own, and then Hashem will help us.

Do small investments really add up to a significant amount? Let us use my Coca Cola stock as an example. Overall, over many years, the stock has grown about 15 percent a year with reinvested dividends, doubling in value approximately every five years. For the last 10 years the growth rate of the stock has been even higher at 24 percent per year. So, let us see what this growth rate can accomplish with an initial investment of only $100, with an additional $10 or other small sum added weekly per family. These are amounts of money that many people can afford.

1. $100 invested in Coca Cola stock 10 years ago, with $10 added weekly, would be worth $22,700 today, based on its 24 percent annual growth this past decade.

2. Even at the more normal annual growth rate of 15 percent, if a *bar mitzvah* boy invests $100 in Coke at age 13, and his parents add $10 weekly, then the investment will be worth $12,500 at age 23, just in time to pay for a wedding and *kollel*. If the same money is left untouched until age 60, compounding at 15 percent for 37 extra years, then it will be worth over $4 million! So, the boy could spend his life contentedly learning Torah, knowing he could have several million dollars available at age 60.

3. If a newlywed *chassan* and *kallah* invest $100 at age 22, and then add $10 weekly, and do not touch the money until age 60, they will have a sum slightly over $1 million.

How encouraging this can be for a newlywed couple! Small investments can grow into large sums if dividends are reinvested, small sums are regularly added and enough time elapses.

4. If $100 is put away in Coca Cola stock for a newborn baby girl, with $10 added weekly, the investment will be worth $68,000 by age 20. What a nice dowry! With only $100 to start and $10 per week!

So you see, small amounts can grow phenomenally if left untouched and if all dividends reinvest in additional fractional shares. This book will specifically lead you to the financially strongest stocks, which have paid constantly rising dividends for endless decades. You can use what you learn from this book to do your own research or just piggyback on the work I have already done. I intend to keep my 22 stocks forever so believe me, I have put my money where my mouth is.

This book will teach you the following things:

1. Spiritual pursuits are more important than the trappings of wealth.

2. A frugal lifestyle applies even to physicians. Living rich doesn't mean you are.

3. The short-term gyrations of the stock market are scary and irrational but over long periods of time the stock market is quite rational and usually very profitable.

4. Buying stock in a well-researched, fundamentally sound and growing company is a logical and fairly safe thing to do.

5. A portfolio should be carefully chosen, diversified properly, and then left alone to grow.

6. Constant trading in and out of the market is neither wise nor profitable, and not a particularly good way for an observant Jew to spend his time.

7. Dividends are absolutely crucial to long-term investing success. This is described in great detail within this book.

Please remember. I retired from full-time medicine at the age of 40 to learn Torah. I did not want to jump from the stress of a medical practice to the stress of full-time investment monitoring. I do not spend a lot of time on my investments. On the contrary, my investments give me the time I need to concentrate on things that really matter, namely, learning Torah and teaching my children.

One final note. It is true that in general these last few years have been excellent times for stock investors. However, my results still beat most mutual funds as I show in the following Introduction. So in extraordinary good times, my hands-off long-term approach beats the actively managed mutual funds. In times that are ordinary, my results will become ordinary as well, but should still be better than actively managed funds. In bad times I expect my results will be poor, but I will probably do better than actively managed funds.

So the fact that these are extraordinary times is irrelevant. The best time to buy stocks was yesterday, the second best time is today, and the next best time is tomorrow. The period we live in is not important, getting in the market early and for the long term is important.

I did not leave my medical practice at age 40 because my stocks recently grew to a large amount. I left because I have faith and confidence that what I have invested in stocks will grow over the next 20 years to support me when I am 60. I retired because of confidence in future growth, not because I was able to hoard a large amount at present. My confidence in future growth gave me the nerve to quit my practice and only work a few nights a week in an emergency room reading X-rays, earning enough to pay the mortgage and the tuition bills. I no longer concern myself with earning inordinate amounts of money to put away for the future, because I believe my stocks will grow enough in the next 20 years to support us. My confidence in the future growth of my stocks also gave me the get up and go to start spending my cash and bond savings at age 40 so I can sit and learn Torah.

It is of utmost importance to note that my scenario is obviously not the norm. I do earn enough part-time to cover major expenses and I did earn enough while I worked full-time to have put away money on which I can draw for immediate expenses. Nevertheless, even if your situation differs drastically from mine and you cannot possibly retire, now is still the time to plan for the future and that is where my plan can prove helpful to you.

A WORD OF CAUTION

n Torah law there is a principle that *punishment* must always be preceded by a warning. In the investing world, I would like to opine that substantial financial *reward* must be preceded by a warning.

This book and this warning should be read carefully. After reading the book, read this warning again, even more carefully. If executed properly the advice contained in this book can lead to many *Baruch Hashems* (on the good, not the bad).

Recently, the stock market took a terrible dip of over 500 points in one day. Somebody asked me a few days later if I had lost money in the dramatic market turbulence. I do not follow the market closely on a daily basis, and I hadn't even known that the Dow had "crashed." I remarked that even if I had lost money, the good news was that my new dividends were being reinvested and buying more shares at a lower price, *Baruch Hashem*. A few days later the market zoomed back upwards, and, unfortunately, my new dividends were now buying shares at a higher price. However, I had gained back much of the substantial money I indeed had lost a few days prior, *Baruch Hashem*.

This book details a conservative, long-term, hands-off approach to stock investing, which is perfect for observant Jews with limited means. It is especially suited for the *bar mitzvah* boy or a new *chassan* and *kallah*. When carried out over a period of many decades, investing as little as $10 a week, substantial wealth even in the millions can be acquired. This can be accomplished with a hands-off approach and very little worry. If the stock market goes up, there is good news concerning growth of principle. If the market goes down, there is good news concerning investing of new capital and reinvested dividends at lower prices. This new money going in at lower prices will often yield the greatest profits decades later. This is the reward. Now for the warnings.

1. PATIENCE

This is a get-rich-slow approach. The optimal time frame for tremendous success is 30-40 years. There will also be reward, perhaps even substantial reward, in 10-20 years. The main reward, however, the explosive exponential growth of capital, occurs only in later years, when reinvested dividends are compounding upon each other again and again, in phenomenal fashion.

2. COMMITMENT

Under no circumstances should anyone ever commit one penny to stocks for 10 minutes under my approach unless they are prepared to hold the stocks for at least 10 years. This rule is ironclad and must be repeated. Do not under any circumstance follow any of the advice in this book unless you will not touch the money for at least 10 years! Period!

3. DO NOT BE GREEDY

Historically, stocks have returned about 10 percent per year, counting reinvested dividends, thus doubling your money every 7 years. There is the occasional wonderful stock like Coca-Cola which has returned about 15 percent per year since 1919, doubling your money every five years. Do not be greedy. Be grateful if you can earn 10-15 percent per year over many decades. Do not grab for quick wealth in risky, untried, volatile investments. That is gambling, not investing.

4. PLAN FOR THE FUTURE

One share of Coke purchased for $42 in 1919 is worth about $5 million today, including reinvested dividends. A 78-year old grandfather given one solitary share as a present on the day of his *bris* (circumcision) in 1919 would have $5 million today to give his family and Torah institutions. If all the yeshivos had gotten together in 1919 and had jointly invested $2,000 in Coke, in a trust to be left untouched for seventy years, the yeshivos today would have $250 million!

5. REINVEST ALL DIVIDENDS

Pick only high-quality conservative American stocks that have paid steadily rising dividends for many decades, even as long as a century. Reinvest every single one of those dividends in additional fractional shares. The fortune from Coke described above would be only one tenth the amount if dividends had not been reinvested! The plan in this book will not work unless all dividends are reinvested in new shares. Dividend reinvestment is free of brokerage commissions, by the way.

6. BE CONSISTENT

Constantly put new money into the same good stocks, over and over again, even $10 per week, in good times and bad. Once you get into the habit of regularly investing small amounts and begin to see how it really adds up, the habit is hard to break.

7. FRUGALITY

Live within your means and invest the savings for the future. You will find that financial freedom is the sweetest thing you have ever bought, and one of the most wonderful things you can ever give to your children.

8. REMAIN CALM

Concentrate on choosing good companies, which is a rational thing. Ignore the stock market's fluctuations, which are irrational. The only rational thing about the gyrations of the market is that over the decades the stock price of a good company will go up and up, closely paralleling the steady rise in the company's profits and dividends. Ignore the short-term ups and downs of the stock market. They are usually meaningless and often not based on the true underlying economic reality of a company. They are based on public emotion and even hysteria. When the market goes up you are rewarded with growth of capital. Be happy. When the market goes down you are rewarded with a low price for your new investments and reinvested dividends. Be happy once again. In the short term, up or down, you win. Long term, if you pick good companies and leave them alone, eventually their prices will rise very, very significantly.

9. HANDS OFF

Be happy, be relaxed, and concentrate on your learning, your family, and your other *mitzvos*. This cannot be stressed enough. Ideally you should start investing at around age 13, or perhaps 20, and then ignore your investments until you are around 60. Pretend Wall Street doesn't exist for a few decades and you will be very, very pleasantly surprised some day when you check your portfolio balance. Following the irrational ups and downs of the market can lead to panic selling, usually at the very worst time.

Choni HaMe'agal once saw a man planting a carob tree. He asked the man why he was bothering, considering it would take 70 years for the tree to mature. The man remarked that he was doing it for his grandchildren. Choni HaMe'agal went to sleep for 70 years and when he awoke he indeed saw that the man's descendants were enjoying the fruits of his labor from many years before. The man's foresight and patience had paid off handsomely for the benefit of his family.

I do not believe that my future grandchildren, *IY"H*, will want an abundance of carob, but they will surely appreciate the fruit of my Coke and other financial plantings many years from now!

INTRODUCTION:
A HOT NEW FUND

The 1997 year end editions of *The Wall Street Journal* and *Investor's Business Daily* have special sections devoted to Mutual Fund performance. Here are some of the statistics compiled by Lipper Analytical Services and Morningstar:

As you can see below, the Meister Funds beat the averages and beat several competing top-notch Fidelity funds.

	1997 RETURN	3-YEAR AVERAGE	5-YEAR AVERAGE
1. AVERAGE DIVERSIFIED US STOCK MUTUAL FUND	25.6%	25.4%	16.7%
2. S&P 500	31%	31.2%	20.3%
3. FIDELITY MAGELLAN FUND	26.6%	24.6%	18.8%
4. FIDELITY CONTRAFUND	23%	26.9%	19.7%
5. FIDELITY BLUE CHIP GROWTH	27%	23.5%	20.8%
6. MEISTER DIVIDEND FUND	33.4%	35.7%	24.7%
7. MEISTER TOTAL FUND	33.1%	37.1%	25.9%

In 1996 the Meister Funds had also topped the charts:

1. AVERAGE DIVERSIFIED US STOCK FUND	19.5%
2. MEISTER DIVIDEND FUND	26.8%
3. MEISTER TOTAL FUND	31%

Wait a second, you say! What are the Meister Funds? They're not listed anywhere in the *Wall Street Journal* or *Money Magazine*, nor are they covered by Lipper Analytical Services or Morningstar. I confess. I sort of snuck them into the tables above. You see, the Meister Fund Family is really the Meister family's funds. And I am the Meister family chief investor, even though our top stock of all time was selected by my wife.

In this book I would like to teach you the simple fundamentals of picking winning long-term stocks. Name-brand familiar stocks. Nothing exotic. Simply high-quality stalwarts of American industry that have paid years of continually rising dividends. I am not Peter Lynch nor Warren Buffett, but their advice and methods apply to me and to everyone. Anyone can select long-term winning stocks with a little careful research and patience.

You may note that I listed two Meister portfolios above. The first, the "Dividend Fund," is one that contains 20 dividend-rich stocks. The second, the "Total Fund,"shows the effect of adding two high-tech "no- or low-dividend"-paying stocks which my wife picked. Even the 20 "boring" dividend-paying stocks beat all the averages. Adding my wife's two spicy stocks boosted the returns a bit. The bulk of our portfolio, and the core on which we truly rely, are the 20 dividend-rich stocks.

In this book I will describe how I went from a medical practice to a *kollel* with dividends. I hope that you will find the whole book useful and instructive. The first seven chapters describe the proper philosophies toward life, and toward investing, that should enable a person to increase the time spent on spiritual pursuits.

Chapters 8 and 9 are perhaps the most important chapters in the book. Chapter 8 describes the absolutely crucial role that dividends play in long-term investing success. Chapter 9 is in effect a practical handbook of fundamental rules of stock analysis.

If you master the information in Chapter 9 then you should be able to pick safe and profitable stocks with confidence. The information in Chapter 9 should be referred to again and again as you analyze stocks for your own portfolio.

The last three chapters describe my own portfolio in detail. Chapter 10 describes the proper balance and diversification that a portfolio should have to be successful. Chapters 11 and 12 describe the specific stocks which I own and which enabled me to retire early and learn Torah. Chapter 12 goes into great detail on each stock, especially details concerning the dividend that each stock pays and its growth over the years. The graphs and charts in this chapter clearly show the tremendous impact of dividend reinvestment on long-term profits. By studying how I selected each of these stocks, you can learn what you need to know to pick other stocks of your own choosing. You may decide to buy some of the same stocks which I have bought. I use a buy-and-hold strategy and I plan on holding these stocks basically forever. However, with the information you learn from this book you will be well prepared to select your own interesting and profitable portfolio.

1

GOING HOME

glanced at my wife Rivka. The sun was shining brightly on her face as she peacefully gazed out the window at the passing Maryland farm country. Our daughter, not even two, was cooing and gurgling contentedly in her car seat in back. She squealed with delight whenever we pointed out "horsies" or "cowsies."

It was June 1, 1996 and we were driving from our home in Baltimore, Maryland to New York City where I grew up. I was 40 years old, and I was retired. Just the day before, May 31, 1996, I had officially resigned my position as a senior partner in a Baltimore radiology practice. The occasion for our trip to New York City was the 20-year reunion of the Ohr Somayach Institute of Jewish Studies which I had attended in Yerushalayim and Monsey during the late 70s having completed both medical school and my internship in pediatrics. I had spent several wonderful years there learning Torah after many grueling years of secular education and before starting several more intense years as a radiology resident.

In retrospect I am not sure that intense even begins to describe my education. I had wanted to be a physician from as early as I could remember. As a kid I did the requisite cute future doctor things of playing with microscopes and doing science experiments at school and even at home. Eventually, as I got older, I took the steps which proved it was more than the usual childhood fascination.

In high school I spent summer vacations working at the New York City Morgue learning anatomy, pathology, and forensics from world-famous pathologist Dr. Milton Helpurn, the chief medical examiner. I also studied under his successor Dr. Michael Baden who was the expert pathologist that testified before congress concerning the Kennedy assasinations. I worked with the FBI one summer helping identify the charred remains of victims of a plane crash at Kennedy Airport. Once, to her horror, my mother discovered that the plastic bucket I kept in my bedroom had contained bodily remains.

This was in the years before I was observant. In the mornings I would read the *New York Daily News* to see whom the Mafia had rubbed out the previous day, which train had crashed, or whatever other gruesome stories I could find, and then go to the morgue and help with the autopsies. I still remember an unfortunate case of an observant storekeeper from the lower East Side who had been murdered by a robber. A Rabbi in a black coat and hat and with a long beard came into the morgue, and supervised the Jew's autopsy. The rabbi made sure that the body was treated with the utmost respect and that the person received a halachic burial. He allowed only the minimum amount of anatomic samples to be taken for subsequent study. I wasn't observant at the time and I knew nothing about halachah (Jewish law), but I was very impressed with the care which the rabbi gave to the dead Jew, and the fact that he was willing to supervise the autopsy in an environment which would be revolting to the nonmedically trained person.

I mentioned above that I knew nothing about halachah. I didn't even know anything about basic Judaism. In my junior year of high school I had a Puerto Rican girl friend (who was also half Polish). We had a date one day in Central Park. We were walking along when she wished me a happy new year. I looked at her with surprise and said that it wasn't New Year's, it was September. She told me that she had read in the newspaper that it was Rosh Hashanah and being I was Jewish she was wishing me a happy new year. In years past the only reason I would know that it was Rosh Hashanah was because New York City public schools were closed for those two days. But Rosh Hashanah this particular year was on a weekend so I hadn't realized that this particular Saturday was the Jewish New Year.

At the same time I was taking up space, literally. I entered a contest sponsored by NASA in 1971 to bring high-school students' experiments onto the Skylab Space Station. Of 4,200 entries, mine was one of 11 experiments chosen to fly aboard Skylab. For the most part NASA wanted student involvement for the publicity value and that aspect certainly paid off for them. It also paid off for me. I was flown by the government to mission control in Houston, to Marshall Space Flight Center in Alabama, and to Cape Kennedy. I was able to witness two blast-offs. I met men who walked on the moon, the men who put them there, and the men who reported on them such as Walter Cronkite and Jules Bergman. I felt privileged to be written up in dozens of newspapers and featured on local and national TV. I still have a TV Guide from June 1972 which lists my name and experiment in the description of a national ABC special on teenage scientists.

In recent years the story of the ill-fated Apollo 13 mission has been told and retold. Jack Lousma, the astronaut who received the famous message, "Houston we have a problem," later flew the space mission on which my experiment was performed, a test which I had devised to study the astronauts' blood during space flight. His autographed photo still hangs on our family room wall, along with those of other astronauts. My children are always thrilled when I point out astronauts whom I have met.

During all this time my single-minded desire to be a physician did not fade. I received my acceptance letter to Albany Medical College in upstate New York in November 1971. The date is unusual in that I was only 16 years old at the time and a senior in high school. The acceptance letter was for the freshman class of 1974 and required that I finish a four-year college program in two years, which I did. I entered medical school at age 18 and proudly held my diploma and M.D. four years later at age 22.

In my second year of medical school I finally realized there was more to life than being a doctor and started developing outside interests. In retrospect, I believe entering medical school at age 18 was a wake up call to my soul. I was on the threshold of a career that people strive for years and years to obtain and I was only 18. I looked around and said to myself, "Is this it?" I figured there had to be more to life than science and career. I started developing interests in art, history, music and other areas I had always ignored. One night in the fall of 1975 I sat down after studying to relax with my dorm mates and watch some TV. Of all things, we future doctors chose to relax with Marcus Welby, M.D., then still a popular prime-time show.

In this particular episode a 19-year-old Jewish boy was dying from a Jewish genetic ailment called sympathetic dysautonomia. Before he died he wanted to have the *bar-mitzvah* ceremony he had never had. According to the story line, his father's being in the camps during the war had turned him anti-religious. Now that the boy was dying he was desperate for a *bar mitzvah*. So of course Marcus Welby helped him, and he was "*bar mitzvah*" before he died. It was a real tear-jerker. Except, I had never had a *bar mitzvah* either. My parents weren't religiously inclined and at age 13 my father offered me the choice of a *bar-mitzvah* ceremony, which would be meaningless to me, or a two-week trip to San Francisco, Hawaii, and Las Vegas. Being a normal 13-year-old male, I chose the trip. While my friends back home became men in synagogue, I became a man by going to a show in Las Vegas.

When the Marcus Welby episode aired, I was in my second year of medical school. I was joking with my friends after the show that I too had never had a *bar mitzvah*. They dared me to have a *bar mitzvah* like the boy in the show. I agreed, because I thought it would be a nice surprise for my mother. Some people are inspired to religion by great rabbis or by inspiring speakers. I was inspired by Robert Young, the gentile actor who portrayed Marcus Welby. I took my roommates up on the dare and to show my enthusiasm I asked if anyone present could teach me a couple of Hebrew letters right there on the spot. No one had a *siddur* or a *Chumash* but a freshman from California was wearing a tee shirt that said hello all over it in dozens of languages. Somewhere on the shirt was the word Shalom in Hebrew letters. My first Hebrew lesson was from my roommate Harold teaching me how to read the word Shalom.

I asked my friends to which synagogue I should go. I had a choice of Orthodox, Conservative, or Reform. I knew that when you compare a liberal to a conservative in politics, the conservative is usually more traditional. So I assumed that Conservative Jews must be the most religious of all three. I wanted to do my *bar mitzvah* right so I figured I would go Conservative. My friends explained to me that the Orthodox were actually more observant than the Conservatives. I didn't believe them, but the closest *shul* to my dormitory was Orthodox so that is where I went.

I showed up that Saturday for services (*Parshas Lech Lecha* 1975) at Congregation Beth Abraham Jacob in Albany, New York. This is a small congregation in upstate New York and a newcomer really stands out. I sort of fumbled along, holding the *siddur* upside down until the *chazzan* (cantor), Sholom Stein z"l, looked at me oddly and turned the *siddur* around in my hands. By the way, this was not the last time that I did unusual things in that *shul*. By the following Yom Kippur I was already observant. I had been told that Jews don't wear leather on Yom Kippur. I thought that applied to belts as well so I left my leather belt home. I spent most of the day desperately holding up my pants with one hand while trying to hold my thick *machzor* (holiday prayer book) with the other.

My ignorance also showed in some of the classes I would later attend. During one class Chazzan Stein taught us that

Shabbos is more important than Chanukah so we must light the *menorah* (candelabrum) before sunset. I had already learned that Yom Kippur was even more important than Shabbos so I raised my hand and asked what happens when Chanukah comes on Yom Kippur? The room went quiet after my question so I figured I must have asked a really good one. You see, I knew that the Jewish holidays always came at different times of the year so I presumed that sometimes Yom Kippur and Chanukah would coincide.

Anyway, after the morning services I went over to the rabbi, Eliezer Langer, and explained that I was a second-year medical student, I was 20, and had never had a *bar mitzvah* and wanted to have one now. He was very nice. He told me to call him during the week and that he would try to help me out.

As I was leaving the synagogue a pleasant middle-aged widow named Bertha Younker approached me and asked me if I would like a Shabbos meal. I had no idea what Shabbos was but I figured I could use a home-cooked meal. I was wearing a shiny blue *yarmulka* which I had from my sister's wedding and from the way Mrs. Younker was talking to me I could tell that she assumed I was observant. I was too embarrassed to tell her that I had no idea what Shabbos was, so I sort of played along until it came time to eat. As she had no husband, and her children were in New York City, she asked me to make *Kiddush*. I looked at her and said, "Mrs. Younker, I have no idea what *Kiddush* is, and even if I did, I couldn't make it if you paid me because I can't read Hebrew." So the cat was out of the bag that I was totally ignorant of *Yiddishkeit*. Mrs. Younker made *Kiddush* for us and we spent an enjoyable afternoon chatting together. It turned out that she had fled Germany as a young girl with her parents and settled in Jackson Heights, New York (a neighborhood in Queens), where coincidentally my parents still lived, and where I had grown up. She was married years ago in the very same neighborhood synagogue where my friends had made their *bar mitzvahs* while I was sneaking into West Coast bars. She explained to me about Shabbos and many other aspects of *Yid-dishkeit.*

The next Friday night I went back to the *shul* and the *chazzan* invited me home for a Friday night Shabbos meal. For the next three years I attended *shul* each weekend and always had a nice Shabbos meal with Mrs. Younker, Chazzan Stein, Rabbi Langer, or other families. To this day, over 20 years later, I can still honestly say that I have never experienced a community who perform the *mitzvah* of *hachnasas orchim* (hospitality) finer than that small *kehillah* (congregation) of Jews in Albany, New York. There were always students in *shul* from local universities and the members of the *shul* would literally fight over us to see who would win the privilege of having a guest. Mrs. Stein once went out in a blizzard on Friday afternoon to buy me a pie she knew I liked. If for some reason I didn't show up, which was rare, I always received a phone call after Shabbos to see if everything was okay. More than one student became observant because of that *kehillah.*

Years later people would ask me what inspired me to Orthodox Judaism. Was it intellectual, like the mind? Or was it emotional, like the heart? I would tell them that it was grumbling, like the stomach. Some people are drawn to religion by the yearnings of their heart, some by the insights of their mind. I was initially drawn by the good Shabbos meals. I was away from home, in an intensive medical program, and the pleasant synagogue services combined with a couple of home-cooked meals were a nice break. I enjoyed meeting the Orthodox families and seeing the beauty of Shabbos glow over parents and children alike. I hadn't given much thought to marriage and family, and had even occasionally made the brash and rather immature statement that I wanted to devote myself to medicine and not have a family. Now I was beginning to rethink things.

Rabbi Langer helped me to prepare to read the *maftir* and the *haftarah* (weekly Scriptural portions) (Shabbos *Rosh Chodesh, Iyar* 1976). One Friday night I went to his home for a Shabbos meal. After a fine meal of chicken with orange sauce, Mrs. Langer brought out ice cream for everyone. I knew nothing

about Judiasm but I vaguely remembered learning that observant Jews don't eat meat and milk at one meal. Now here was
ice cream served right on the table with the chicken. I figured
that I had been wrong about the one thing which I thought I
knew about Judiasm. Mrs. Langer asked me what I would like
to drink with my dessert so I asked for a glass of milk. The table
went silent and everyone stared at me. Mrs. Langer told me that
I can't have milk after chicken. I said, "Well, the Rabbi is having
ice cream with his!" That night I learned about *pareve* ice
cream.

Between my first visit to *shul* in October 1975 and my *bar
mitzvah* ceremony in May 1976, I slowly became observant.
I did things gradually. Usually people can tell if a person prac-
tices trustworthy *kashrus* by whether or not he keeps
Shabbos. Well, I enjoyed Shabbos so much that I started ob-
serving it before I was even keeping kosher! I was not
carrying in public on Saturday but still eating ham! My
kashrus observance came slowly. First I stopped eating pork,
lobster, etc. but I would still eat *treifah* (nonkosher) beef.
Then I stopped mixing milk and meat. My *bar-mitzvah* ceremony was rapidly approaching, right after Pesach 1976. I
figured that for Pesach I would get new dishes and start keeping kosher.

My dorm mates knew I was contemplating changing to full
kashrus observance for Pesach. So the night before Pesach
they took me out to my favorite nonkosher Chinese restaurant
in Albany and each one bought me one of my favorite *treif* dishes — shrimp with lobster sauce, pork spareribs, etc. — for one
last totally *treifah* experience. The next day I switched to eating
nothing but kosher food.

I celebrated my *bar mitzvah* in May 1976. I proudly read from
the Torah and *haftarah* in Hebrew. My father had never had a
bar-mitzvah ceremony either. He too learned to read Hebrew
and we made a joint ceremony in the packed *shul*. On this particular Shabbos the *shul* was even more packed than usual. I
had invited my entire medical school class. One of the older
women in *shul* kept wondering aloud how there could be so

many Jews in my medical school, somehow not noticing that a good deal of the crowd which had showed up was Asian, African American, or blonde with blue eyes. Some Jews showed up as well!

After my "*bar mitzvah*" I was *shomer mitzvos* (observant of the commandments). This took a certain amount of *mesiras nefesh* (self-sacrifice). In medical training a person often is required to work in the hospital on Friday nights and Saturdays. In the very beginning I would sometimes do medical work on Shabbos, but I tried my best to limit it to very sick patients or rabbinic *melachos* (proscribed labors), according to the level of halachah I was able to understand in those days. I would even pay a gentile medical student to accompany me to do my writing, drawing blood, etc. In one pediatric department there was an Italian secretary named Maria who wore a big cross around her neck. She would often answer phones or write on Shabbos for me. Then one day she told me that she knew all about Judaism because her mother was Jewish! *Oy vei*! My *Shabbos Goy* was a Jew!

Soon after that I figured it was more prudent to stop working on Shabbos altogether, and I did. I would trade shifts with gentiles and I would work two Sundays in a row or some similar arrangement to avoid working on Shabbos. Toward the end of my internship I could not find anyone to cover the second day of Shavuos for me. I told the chief resident in pediatrics that I couldn't work that day. He said I had to or I was fired. So I quit, two weeks away from completing my internship and receiving my medical license. I was about to throw away almost a decade of hard work and my entire career, but I was no longer going to desecrate Shabbos or Yom Tov. *Baruch Hashem*, they called me back a few days later and allowed me to complete my internship.

One Friday night during the period that I was still working on Shabbos I was told that there was an elderly nonobservant Jewish lady in one of the hospital rooms. She was in a very advanced stage of Alzheimer's and recognized no one, and more or less was totally oblivious to her surroundings. I was sort of lonely spending Friday night in the hospital so I decided to make *Kiddush* in her room. After I finished the last *berachah* she opened her eyes and said, in a loud and clear voice, "Amen!" Then she closed her eyes again and was totally out of it. I think of it to this day. You just never know how a *mitzvah* may affect someone.

One day while I was working at the Veterans Hospital in Albany I came across an elderly Jewish man sitting in a wheelchair in the x-ray department. He was wearing a black velvet *yarmulka* and looking lonely. I knew that he was not from our community in Albany. He told me that he lived in a little village way out in the middle of nowhere called Sharon Springs. He was not married and had no children. During the summer months other observant Jews would vacation there but most of the year he was just about the only observant Jew around. He was having trouble getting kosher food at the VA hospital so my wife would cook him chicken soup or fish and I would bring it to him. I eventually managed to get the hospital to provide him with kosher meals.

From outward appearances and from the way he talked he seemed to be a poor man. Eventually he was discharged and returned to Sharon Springs. One day a *meshulach* (charity collector) from Mesivta Tifereth Jerusalem came to stay at my house in Albany. He asked me if I knew a man way out in the country in Sharon Springs from whom he wanted to solicit a large donation. He mentioned the name of my patient. To my amazement it turned out that the "poor" man was a multimillionaire who owned most of the land in Sharon Springs. To this day I harbor a secret fantasy that someday he will leave me all his millions in his will because I helped him when I thought that he was nothing but a poor, lonely Jew. That was almost 15 years ago. Some fantasies die hard.

Around this time, I started wearing a *yarmulka* in the medical center. I had no problem with this during the daytime hours. The problem was at night. Several times a month I was required to sleep over in a hospital on-call room and be available for emergencies such as cardiac arrests (heart attacks) and the like. The hospital page operator would ring the phone in my on-call room and tell me where in the hospital I would have to run to in order to help save a patient's life. Every second counted so I worked on reflex, like a fireman. When the phone rang I would wake up, grab my clothes and shoes, and run.

The problem was, I was still not used to wearing a *yarmulka*. My reflexes were not attuned to automatically grabbing my *yarmulka* before I ran out of my room, so I often ran off without it. One night as I went to sleep in my on-call room I repeated the following mantra to myself, "Take the *yarmulka*, take the *yarmulka*, take the *yarmulka*." At 2 A.M. my phone rang. I bolted upright in bed. Cardiac arrest! I grabbed my *yarmulka* and ran. My presleep mantra had worked. As I ran down the hospital corridor I reached my hand up to my head. Yes! My *yarmulka* was securely in place. Then I looked down. I had forgotten my pants! Thank G-d no one died during the 20 seconds it took me to run back and get my pants. Later that night, as I fitfully tried to fall back asleep, I could be heard mumbling to myself, "*Yarmulka*, then pants. *Yarmulka*, then pants. *Yarmulka*, then pants."

During those years I was slowly beginning to realize that learning Torah was the cornerstone of all of Judaism. There were various classes that I was able to attend at the *shul* and at people's homes. In addition to learning on my own, I would try to buttonhole people, whenever I could, to learn with me. There was an observant professor of microbiology at Albany Medical College and he learned *Chumash* and *Rashi* with me daily during lunch. I was once walking through the hospital in the middle of the night when I saw a *chassid* with long *peyos* and wearing a long black coat sitting in the hall. That may be common at Maimonides Hospital in Boro Park but it is not your usual sight at Albany Medical Center. It turned out that his daughter had been in involved in a serious car accident in upstate New York and had been taken to Albany Medical Center Hospital. She was in the ICU for weeks, was in a coma for a while, had multiple operations, but eventually made a full recovery. Years later I danced at her wedding in Williamsburg, Brooklyn. So I went over to her father and introduced myself and asked him if he would teach me Torah. I was doing a dermatology rotation at the time and had some free time for learning (*Baruch Hashem*, there aren't too many emergency pimples). He agreed and taught me *Parshas Vayikra* with *Rashi*. I spent the following Pesach at his house in Williamsburg, and was privileged to meet the Satmar Rebbe *zt"l* on the last Pesach of his life.

Yaakov Levinson who wrote *The Jewish Guide to Natural Nutrition* was a nutritionist in Albany during this period. He would learn with me and he lent me Torah tapes on Mishnah *Berachos*. I did not have a tape recorder but the medical school library had a multimedia center which had tape recorders and slide projectors. Each night I would check out a carousel of medical slides from the library reference desk and reserve a multimedia room. Then I would go upstairs and learn *mishnayos*. Nobody caught on. Then one day I received a letter from the head librarian saying she needed to speak to me about my use of the multimedia center. I figured that the jig was up and now I would be in trouble for using medical library tape recorders to listen to Torah tapes. It turned out that some potentially generous donors were coming to visit the medical center. The library had researched their files and discovered that I checked out more slides than any other medical student. They wanted me to speak to the donors about our wonderful library, seeing that I used the place more often than any other student. Needless to say, I told the gentile donors what a wonderful multimedia center Albany Medical College provided for their students. I neglected to mention that I only used it for learning Torah.

I would catch smatterings of Torah whenever I could. During a surgery rotation in my senior year of medical school I would assist senior surgeons while they performed operations but there would often be breaks when I was not needed. I would keep a linear *Chumash* with *Rashi* open on a stool behind me and during such breaks I would turn away from the operating table and learn *Chumash*. I was wearing a surgical gown and sterile gloves so the nurse would turn the pages for me when I was ready.

Even though I was observant, I was still a bit of a wise guy. Once a senior surgeon was removing a tumor from someone's colon and as he was taking the specimen to put it into a pathology basin it slipped out of his hands and plopped right onto the operating-room floor! Everyone was shocked but no one had the temerity to say anything to a senior surgeon. I piped up and asked, "Excuse me sir, how often does this particular form of cancer spread to the linoleum?"

I was once performing a breast biopsy with the Chairman of Surgery. He was very mean tempered and fastidious and wouldn't let students do very much to help him. To everyone's surprise he offered to let me cut his sutures as he tied knots within the patient. This was not as easy as it sounds. If the thread is cut too long then the ends will irritate the inside of the breast and lead to infection. If the thread is cut too short, then the knot can come undone and the patient can bleed. So I cut one and he said "Too short." I would cut another one and he would say "Too long." This went on for many minutes. "Too short." "Too long." "Too short." "Too long." No matter what I did he wasn't satisfied. Finally, I put down my scissors and said, "Look, make up your mind. Do you want them too short or too long?" He threw me out of the operating room.

In 1977 my Torah learning took a big turn for the better. There was a renowned *talmid chacham* (Torah scholar) who lived in Albany. His name was Rabbi Zalman Levine *z"l*. He was the son of a famous *tzaddik* who had been known as the "*Malach*." There is a published collection of letters from the *Malach* to his son in Albany which makes excellent *mussar* reading. To this day there is a *Malach Kollel* in Monsey. R' Zalman knew all of Talmud by heart. Once on Shavuos he left the shul at midnight and returned at 4 A.M. We all found this surprising. We figured that of all people R' Zalman would certainly stay up all night learning. When he returned we asked him why he had left at midnight and then returned at 4 A.M. He looked at us and said, "That's what I do every night." In Albany, New York of all places someone was learning Torah all night every night!

R' Zalman was an elderly man. On Yom Kippur of 1977 he

suffered a heart attack while in *shul.* I performed CPR and accompanied him to the hospital. He eventually recovered fully and lived many more years. While recuperating in intensive care he would learn *Chumash* with me. During *Chol HaMoed* (the Intermediate Days of) *Succos,* one of R' Zalman's former *talmidim* (students), Yirmiyahu Luchins, while visiting his parents, came to visit him in the hospital. R' Zalman introduced us and Yirmiyahu literally changed my life. He had a PhD in chemistry and was a brilliant scientist, yet he spent most of his time learning Torah. Today he works not as a scientist but as a *rebbi* in a day school. After he returned home to Washington Heights he would call me regularly and we would learn *mishnayos* together on the phone. He was my first role model of a professional who put Torah learning ahead of his career. He would always tell me that if he left chemistry there would be more than enough non-Jews to fill his place. But if he left the *beis midrash* (study hall) there was no one to fill his place. Those words penetrated me like an arrow and they guide my life to this day.

My father, of course, was not observant. He would tell me, "Look. Your medical career is concrete. It is real. The Torah is not definitely real. G-d may or may not exist. So why throw away something concrete for something that is only a maybe?" Years later I was studying at Ohr Somayach in Yerushalayim. One day I asked one of my *rebbes,* a fiery Gerer *chassid* named Rabbi Avraham Mordechai Isbee, if I should continue my Torah studies or return to medicine. I had never told him nor anyone else what my father had told me. Rabbi Isbee looked at me and said "Look. The Torah and Hashem are real. They are concrete. Your medical career is a maybe. You may make money and you may not. So why throw away something concrete for something that is only a maybe?"

After my internship in pediatrics I took three years off from my medical studies and learned Torah full time at Ohr Somayach in Jerusalem and Monsey, New York as well as at Yeshivah Kol Yaakov in Monsey with my Rosh Yeshivah, Rabbi Leib Tropper. I married while at Ohr Somayach in Jerusalem and the first of my five children was born there.

Before my wedding I went to Rabbi Shach in Bnei Brak for a *berachah*. He asked where I was learning. When I told him that I was learning at Ohr Somayach in Jerusalem he asked me how I became observant. I told him the whole story about becoming *frum* from a television show. He exclaimed in Hebrew, "From television!? This is the first time I have ever heard that something good came from television." Over and over again he kept repeating in Hebrew, "*Min hateleviziah*? *Min hateleviziah*?" Apparently my story made quite an impression on Rabbi Shach. A few weeks later my *rebbi*, Rabbi Aharon Feldman, came over to me and told me that he had regards for me from Bnei Brak. I told him that I didn't know anybody in Bnei Brak. He told me that he had gone to Rabbi Shach with a *she'eilah* (question of Jewish law) and that when Rabbi Shach heard that my *rebbi* taught at Ohr Somayach he told him to give regards to the *bachur* (boy) who became observant from television!

I also went to the Steipler for a blessing before my wedding. He gave me one and then I bought two of his books. He smiled at me and said, "*Me'ah v'esrim*." I assumed that this was a further blessing that I should live and be well until 120 years so I smiled back. He smiled again and said, "*Me'ah v'esrim*." Once again I nodded and smiled back. This went on a few more times until I realized that he was telling me that the two books cost 120 Israel *Lire* (this was in the days before the *shekel*). I quickly paid and left. I remember thinking that if this had gone on much longer, and that if I would have kept the *tzaddik hador* (foremost sage of his generation) from his learning any longer with my 120 mix-up, the universe may have ceased to exist or some other catastrophe may have occurred. I also received blessings from the previous Gerer Rebbe and from the Lelover Rebbe but *baruch Hashem* I did not make a fool of myself in front of them.

I was very, very happy during these years. I knew that someday I would want to return to full time Torah studies. Yirmiyahu Luchins was right. No one would miss me in the hospital. But who could replace a Jew in the *beis midrash*? During these yeshivah years I occasionally practiced medicine, helping out the members of the yeshivah community when they needed it.

Once during my stay in Israel I needed medical help myself.

Like many in that country I contracted hepatitis. There is a famous pigeon cure for hepatitis which is often utilized in *Eretz Yisrael*. A pigeon's backside is placed on the patient's belly button. The pigeon mysteriously dies and the patient suddenly gets better. This cure is widely used in the observant community, even sneaking pigeons into hospitals. I was willing to try it. A number of pigeons is used which matches one's blood bilirubin level. The bilirubin level in a normal person is less than 1. A person with hepatitis can have a bilirubin of 5-10. Mine was near 40, almost fatal! So a doctor brought me 40 pigeons from Bnei Brak. They cost $10 each. I asked him if Blue Cross would cover them. He told me not to even bother submitting the paperwork. Well, on Erev Pesach, after *bedikas chametz* (search for leaven), the doctor placed 40 pigeons on my navel and, sure enough, they died one after the other. For a test he would touch a pigeon to my arm or to the floor and nothing would happen. As soon as the poor little bird would sit on my navel it would die. Only male pigeons are effective for male patients and female pigeons for female patients. Pigeon #8 would not die. Further inspection revealed it to be a female, so we set her free. Well, we finally finished and I was still sick, except now I also had 39 dead pigeons in my bedroom and my belly was covered with pigeon feathers and other dirt.

Next I had all the *mezuzos* checked in our apartment. There was a door leading from the master bedroom to the *succah* porch. Apparently rainwater had gotten into that *mezuzah* case and the *mezuzah* on the room where I slept had become moldy and had turned BRIGHT YELLOW! And I was bright yellow from hepatitis. We changed the *mezuzos* and still I did not get better.

More weeks passed and I was still not getting better. I had constant nausea with no appetite and I had lost 50 pounds. My wife was expecting during my illness and one night she went into labor and we were blessed with a baby boy. Just before going into labor and leaving for the hospital my wife had cooked a large pot of noodles. While she was in the hospital I ate the whole pot. It was the first time I had eaten well in months. I figured that the excitement of the new baby must have given me an appetite for the bland noodles. The next day a neighbor brought a big plate of fatty chicken. I ate that too. With hepatitis your liver does not function properly and you usually cannot even look at greasy foods, much less eat them. From that moment on my appetite returned, my weight increased, and I felt better. At my son's *bris* (circumcision) I mentioned to a Rabbi that when the baby was born I seemed to feel better. He told me about a *Yerushalmi* in *Moed Kattan* (3:7) where it is written, "*Im nolad ben zachar, b'oisah hamishpacha, nisra'peis kol oisah hamishpachah*" (When a baby boy is born, the whole family is healed)!

Now, many years later, my wife and I were driving to New York City from Baltimore to attend the Ohr Somayach reunion. It was six weeks before my 41st birthday! I had reached my goal with a month and a half to spare. I still have to do some part-time work. I read x-rays in a local emergency room a few nights a week to supplement my investment income and make ends meet. When I first started dreaming of retiring to learn Torah we had one child, not yet in school, and we somehow managed to live quite comfortably on my resident's salary of around $20,000 a year. By age 40 we had four children, a fifth on the way, and we were paying three yeshivah tuitions, with at least two Beis Yaakov tuitions coming up. Still, even with a bigger family, with more expenses, and with inflation, I was able to pare down my medical work to a fraction of what it used to be and begin learning Torah as my main career. The medicine I do practice now is less stressful and more satisfying.

We did it by being frugal. We did it by careful, conservative investing. We did it with dividends! I carefully researched stocks for a full year and then purchased, over a period, a portfolio of 22 solid, growing, dividend-paying stocks. This portfolio has grown enough to allow me to learn Torah by age 40. My yearly and annualized returns for the past five years have exceeded the Dow Jones, the S&P 500, and almost all mutual funds, including many Fidelity stars. After reading this book you should have learned what you need to know to begin selecting stocks for your own portfolio. But there are some lessons about investing, and life, which don't come from books. They come from home, even from a nonreligious home.

2

BEING HOME

t was both ironic and fitting that my Ohr Somayach reunion was on the first day of my new career in Torah learning. And it was even more ironic and fitting that we were going to spend the night in New York at my parents' apartment. It was the same two-bedroom apartment that they had lived in for almost 40 years the apartment in which I had grown up. My parents were satisfied with a modest place to live, had never spent a lot of money to "move on up," and had always lived within their means. They had trained me well by example.

My wife and I arrived at my parents' home. We were going to leave our baby daughter with them before heading into Brooklyn for our reunion. Rivka grew up in a roomy and comfortable traditional southern colonial home in Richmond, Virginia. She and her three siblings had their own bedrooms, a backyard, and a big magnolia tree in the front yard. Whenever we stay at my parents, my wife marvels at the difference in our childhood homes and is always amazed at the simple apartment that was home to me for so many years.

My parents' apartment, a co-op actually, is quite typical of New York apartments, and is actually roomier than many. It is less than 1,000 square feet with a kitchen barely large enough for my petite mother. There are only two bedrooms. The smaller bedroom was made even smaller by a partition down the middle to afford some privacy to me and my sister, as we had to make do with one room for the two of us. The only place for privacy when talking on the phone was to stretch the cord into the hallway bathroom. There were two bathrooms but only one bathtub. We did not have a magnolia tree or indeed any sort of tree at all. We had a concrete playground across the street.

But we also had a lot of love and a feeling of satisfaction. To be honest, I never really felt that our apartment was small. My parents never complained. They dressed nicely but not too expensively. My father never bought the latest, most fashionable clothing. He used to joke that some of his clothes were so old fashioned that every decade or so they came back into style. Who cared? I didn't. He didn't. He was happy living within his means.

My father did not retire from a lucrative medical practice. He grew up in Brooklyn, New York during the depression. His parents were tailors in the garment district like many of their Jewish immigrant peers. Like most American Jews, my great-grandparents had been observant in Europe. Each of my grandmothers kept a kosher home even in America. My father never completed college. Over the years he worked at successive jobs as a clerk, a salesman, and finally a division manager for an insurance company. My mother stayed home to care for my sister and me until we were in high school and then she went to work in various secretarial positions. They put my sister through college and me through medical school. I had a few school loans, but the bulk of the expense was paid for by my parents.

My parents were frugal but not insanely so. The apartment was small. Their clothes were somewhat outdated. The furniture was a mix of old and new, but nice and solid, mostly purchased after their wedding in 1950. But my sister and I were well educated. We had lovely vacations. We often dined in restaurants. We led a simple but comfortable existence.

Any income my father didn't spend for daily expenses he put into conservative investments, with either interest or dividends compounding. He always told me that compound interest was the eighth wonder of the world. When someone asked Albert Einstein what was the most amazing thing that he had ever observed, he answered, "Compound interest." In fact, if the Native Americans who received $24 for the island of Manhattan in 1626 had invested it at 5 percent compound annual interest, it would be worth over $1 billion today. If they had invested it instead in stocks averaging 10 percent a year, they would have countless trillions; to be exact, they would have $24 with 15 zeros after it.

As I sit in my parents' small but comfortable apartment in June 1996 I see a happy couple that didn't squander their hard-earned money and now can enjoy their golden years traveling, visiting their nine grandchildren, or taking marathon walks. Their lessons have brought me here at age 40. I am almost completely retired from medicine. I am about to start pursuing my dream of learning Torah.

I should mention that my in-laws are also responsible parents especially when it comes to living decent lives and passing on worthwhile lessons to their children. I could not begin to live out my dreams without the help of my wife Rivka. She supported and encouraged my decision to leave my lucrative medical practice for the simpler life of learning. She married a physician but she is much happier being the wife of a *kollel* man. My father-in-law has a PhD in physics and holds several patents. Yet when he was in his 40s he became a *baal teshuvah*. Both he and my mother-in-law made many sacrifices to become observant and maintain a kosher home in Richmond, Virginia. By living example they gave over to my wife and her siblings the lesson that there is more to life than career and money while teaching them the importance of Torah. My father-in-law just completed the Babylonian Talmud for the first time. He completed the last page of Tractate *Niddah* and waited for the international *Daf Yomi siyum* to read the final words.

My parents and in-laws both continue to enjoy their golden years and my wife and I are about to start ours. My father's lessons have brought me to this happy stage in my life. Live simply. Live within your means. Stress education. Save and save and save. Be conservative in your investments. Let the interest compound. Set up a steady stream of growing dividend income.

My father accomplished his life's dreams on what he says was never a particularly large salary. During my three years of radiology residency training I made around $20,000 per year. During four years of part-time work immediately following the completion of my medical training I made between double and quadruple that. It was only in the last six years that I have worked full time as a physician and made a typical doctor's salary.

I am aware that these figures are considerably higher than the earnings of many families, nonetheless it is still possible to save and invest on any scale.

Don't think that only rich people can achieve financial freedom. My father did it by living the simple life. I did it in 13 years as a full-and part-time physician. Middle-class people can become secure. And rich doctors can be a lot poorer than you think.

3

POOR PHYSICIAN

P eople who read this book may think that it is easy for a physician to retire at age 40. After all, he IS a doctor and we all know the huge amounts of money that a doctor can make. First of all, with the advent of managed care and HMO's, with ever increasing Medicare and Medicaid cutbacks, as well as a myriad of other problems, doctors no longer make quite the huge amounts of money they used to. That's not the point. I was in medicine during some of the more lucrative years and I did very well. But that's not why I am able to retire at age 40. Many of my peers earned much, much more than I ever did. They are not retired, nor can they retire. And some of them are 60 or older!

How's that again? Physicians have worked full time for 30 years during the true golden years of medical incomes, and they can't retire? Why on earth not? Because they lived like doctors all those years. There is a big difference between spending and saving; flashing wealth and accumulating wealth. Many of the physicians I have worked with have extremely opulent homes. Sometimes they spend money on a new home every three to five years just for pleasure and the thrill of constantly moving further and further up the scale. Some have million-dollar homes with corresponding mortgages. Many have one or more vacation homes. They wouldn't think twice about blowing ten grand on a short vacation.

They drove the most luxurious of cars — Mercedes, Jaguars, Lexuses, and Corvettes. They got new cars every two years, solely for fun. I knew one physician whose cars were worth more than my home. I worked with one doctor who had bought an extremely expensive car. He would complain that he wasn't all that happy with its size and performance. I asked him why he bought it. He said that he liked the fact that people stared at him and his car with envy when he stopped for a red light. My goodness! I drive a midsize Ford. If I really wanted people to stare, I could drive it while wearing a lime-green *yarmulka* that says "Look At Me" in purple letters. That way I could get the stares at red lights without spending $100,000. This very same doctor told me that his DAILY expense on principle and interest on his various mortgages, car leases, etc., was $300 — just on loan payments! This is before paying for food and other necessities. That doesn't leave much left over for investing, even on a doctor's salary.

These physicians never really invested seriously because they all thought the gravy train would last forever and somehow retirement would take care of itself. If they did invest, it was often in crazy, hard-to-understand limited partnerships or exotic-sounding initial public offerings of risky technology stocks or other fad investments. These were investments made on hot tips without having done any fundamental research. They figured that they were smart enough to be doctors and therefore they were smart enough to figure out really cool and complicated investments. At work, nurses, staff, and even patients jumped at their every command.

They reckoned that their investments would also obey "doctor's orders" and go up, up, up.

More than one had a comeuppance when he or she realized that unlike underlings in a hospital, risky investments do not follow orders. Many realized too late that just because one was smart enough to be a physician doesn't mean he knows anything about investing. To be fair, physicians are usually very very busy and really don't have time for investment reading. They work 10-hour days and sometimes they work 24-hour days. Or 48 hour days. They can stay up through the night a few times a week and are in stressful situations with sick and dying people. It is all they can do to master the latest professional and technical literature. There is not a lot of time remaining for friends or family, much less for investment education.

But the main culprit keeping my colleagues from true longtime financial security is the lifestyle of spend, spend, spend. They assumed that wealth meant living wealthy. It doesn't. Wealth comes from saving and investing and living simply. The average millionaire in America is not Donald Trump. The middle-class person or physician who lives like Donald Trump is usually sitting in a pretty fragile house of cards, with a foundation of leases, debt, and interest payments. The trappings of wealth are there but there are no long-term savings or security to back it up. The average millionaire in America (and there are several million) lives in a simple house in a small town. He drives an old car. He has been married to the same woman for his whole life. He owns a simple business and still works hard. The average millionaire does not live like a millionaire. Sam Walton, billionaire founder of WalMart, drove a beat-up pickup truck until the day he died. Warren Buffett, the billionaire from Omaha, has lived in the same small house for 40 years.[1]

I knew years ago that I wanted to retire early and learn Torah full time. I had a few strong things in my favor. I had my parents' lessons of frugality. My wife is loving, supportive, practical, and frugal. I had the ability to harness a physician's

---

1. For further instructive reading on this point you may want to read the new book, *The Millionaire Next Door*, by Thomas J. Stanley and William D. Danko.

earning power for a few good years. Most importantly, I had the good sense not to blow this opportunity. I wanted to make a few good years of high earnings last a lifetime. I wanted a safe, conservative, secure, long-term investment plan that would carry me through a lifetime. I wanted investments that could run on automatic pilot while I learned Torah, perhaps while living again in *Eretz Yisrael* far away from the *Wall Street Journal* and my broker's telephone.

Eleven years ago I started learning how to invest. I read the popular magazines such as *Money, Kiplinger's, Business Week* and *Forbes*. I read the *Wall Street Journal* daily. I had learned nothing but medical studies since childhood and knew absolutely zero about investing. When I was first married I didn't even know how to balance a checkbook or buy a bank CD. After learning the basics of investments, I then turned to specific vehicles.

I spent a few hours a week for about a year perusing through Value Line Investment Survey in the public library and even invested $65 on a 13-week subscription for the home. Value Line lists 1700 stocks with 15 years of historical data on each, virtually everything you could want to know about the stock. It gives overviews of whole industries and compares individual stocks within industries.

I selected 22 diversified stocks which I felt would go up over the long haul and which were safe enough to ignore over long periods. My picks were successful enough to allow me to retire. Obviously I have had a good bull market to help me. But the whole country has had the same bull market as I did. Still, in the last five to seven years I have exceeded the yearly and annualized five-year returns of the Dow, the S&P 500, and most mutual funds including Magellan and other Fidelity stars.

I have done it with no annual fees and with minuscule brokerage and tax costs. And mostly with dividends. Good, solid companies that have paid rising dividends for 50-100 years. My father had the good fortune of a steady stream of "dividends" when his clients would continually renew their insurance policies. But in my medical practice patients only paid for their x-rays once, if at all. So I needed a different source of dividend income — from stocks.

In the next chapters I will tell you how the stock-dividend strategy works for me, works for others, and can work for you. I will explain how I picked my 22 stocks which I plan to hold forever. You can pick the same ones or use your own skills to pick others. My success also relies on living frugally and having some balance in my portfolio from bonds and cash equivalents. I will leave learning the details of how to live a frugal life and how to properly balance a portfolio with bonds and cash for you to learn from other authors.

(You may want to read *The Tightwad Gazette* by Amy Dacyczyn or *Starting Small, Investing Smart* by Don Nichols.)

I do not know how to pick a stock that will go up tomorrow, next week, or even this year, and I'm not sure anybody does. But I can teach you how to pick stocks that will reward you 10, 20 and 30 years down the line. You will learn that downs in the stock market are buying opportunities for new money or for your reinvesting dividends. You will learn the difference between stocks and the "stock market." You will see that you, the individual, can be more successful than the professional money managers who run mutual funds.

4

BUDGETING TIME FOR TORAH

Editor's note: In this chapter, the author describes his own novel approach to learning. It is sharply at variance with standard yeshivh curricula, and it is certainly not suitable for a structured yeshivah setting, but it has much to recommend it. It is based on two concepts: (1) After one has accumulated a broad foundation of factual knowledge, one can then proceed to learn in depth. Facts are the tools of understanding; the more knowledge one has, the better he can build. (2) A scheduled, daily regimen forces one to marshall time and concentration. As the Daf Yomi program proves, a strict, inviolable schedule succeeds.

Dr. Tuvia Meister here describes his own journey and program. He freely acknowledges that his program depended on a somewhat superficial learning for many years, but he found that it provided him with the basis for more intensive learning. Is it for everyone? No. A look at his program will demonstrate that very quickly. But it surely can be of great benefit to many people, and the basic philosophy can be adapted to more moderate programs to suit the needs and schedules of individuals.

T he remainder of this book discusses how to make financial plans and budgets. I thought it would be appropriate to first explain how to make Torah plans and budgets.

It was a glorious fall day in 1979. The beautiful sound of Torah learning rang out from the small classroom, echoing off into the Jerusalem hills just beyond the open window. The students at Yeshivah Ohr Somayach were having a heated discussion about conspiring witnesses (*eidim zomemim*), which had come up as a side point to a *Tosafos* in *Bava Basra*. I was really enjoying the excitement, and the give and take of the discussion, when it slowly dawned on me that I had no idea what these false witnesses were, which laws applied to them, or how they worked. I had been religious for almost four years, and had just started my first full year in yeshivah, the beginning of a three-year hiatus from my medical training. My technical skills in *Gemara* were pretty good and enabled me to more or less work my way from the top of the page to the bottom, figuring out where questions ended, where answers began, and other purely mechanical processes. But my overall knowledge of Torah facts, my fund of knowledge, was still very, very weak.

This was a familiar problem for me. I was often frustrated by the seemingly insurmountable task before me — learn to read Hebrew, learn to understand Hebrew, learn the verb conjugations, learn the basics of Torah, learn the mechanics of Torah, and then .....learn Torah! Several times during the previous four years I had attended lectures at Yeshivah Sh'or Yoshuv in New York during medical-school breaks and vacations. I had grown close to the Rosh Yeshivah, Rabbi Shlomo Freifeld *zt'l*. Back in

1976, he had recommended that I spend a few years translating *Chumash* with *Rashi* before tackling more difficult areas of learning. It was wonderful advice. He instilled in me the idea that I should be patient, and slowly work my way up the hierarchy of Torah learning.

Now in Jerusalem, I expressed my frustrations to my *rebbi*, Rabbi Aharon Feldman , and he was very understanding. I told him that I didn't want to attempt to expound deep Talmudic ideas when in reality I still did not know the fundamental facts or principles behind most areas of Torah learning. He explained that a yeshivah like Ohr Somayach has to show a previously nonreligious person, who often possesses a high level of secular education and a good intellect, the intricacies and depths of Talmudic learning or he may lose interest and return to the challenge of his secular studies instead. That was why in-depth discussions were often pursued early on, even though the students may still be lacking basic knowledge of Torah. At this point I felt that I was committed to pursuing my Torah studies. I did not think that hitting the books and starting at the bottom would turn me off. To the contrary, I was seeking an approach that would teach me the basics so that I could better enjoy more advanced learning in later years.

Rabbi Feldman suggested that I drop out of his class and spend the year learning *Mishnayos*. I followed his advice and spent that year, my first full year in yeshivah, learning all 523 chapters of *Mishnayos*. I learned each with *Bartenura,* using *Tiferes Yisrael* and *Kehati* when needed. My *kallah* suggested that I take notes as I learned, as a study aid. I summarized the entire *Mishnayos* in English. I cross-referred similar areas and organized various areas of learning into sub-topics, such as the five things that invalidate *shechitah* (ritual slaughter), ten things that invalidate a *get* (bill of divorce), the categories of *treifos* (defects that render an animal nonkosher), when a person must return lost property, etc. Then in later years, using my notes, I could usually find which *mishnayos* discussed the material I needed. This would then lead me to the appropriate place in *Gemara* or *Shulchan Aruch* to learn the topic in greater depth. During this first full year in yeshivah, I also learned through all of Tractates *Shabbos* and *Berachos* with *Rashi,* and wrote notes summarizing them in English.

It was hard to be learning on a different track from everyone else. Sometimes I had my doubts if I was doing the right thing, going against the normal order of the yeshivah. Occasionally, incidents occurred during my year of learning *Mishnayos* which would encourage me. For example, I had been learning the sixth chapter of *Talmud Berachos,* when I came to the discussion of which blessing a person makes upon eating an edible fruit peel. A proof is brought from the peel of *orlah* fruit. I had already learned that it is forbidden to eat even the peel of *orlah* fruit (*Orlah* 1:8). Therefore this *Gemara* made no sense to me; it was contradicting a *Mishnah* in *Orlah.* I looked all over for an answer (*Tosafos, Maharsha, Rosh,* etc.) to no avail. Then I turned the page, and the very first words on the top of the *amud* were "*Meis'vei*...we have a question" and the *Gemara* proceeded to ask my question from the very *Mishnah* I quoted. It felt good to have questioned the contradiction before having seen it raised by the *Gemara.*

Another time there was a discussion in the *beis midrash* concerning a sacrificial animal (*korban*) that had died without benefit of ritual slaughter. We were trying to figure out if one can make use of the skin of the dead animal. Someone said, "If an animal has a blemish (*mum*) you can use the skin, and what could be a bigger blemish than death itself, so certainly you can use the skin of a dead animal!" There was only one problem. I had already learned in *Chullin* (10:2) and *Bechoros* (2:2,3), that it is unequivocally forbidden to use the skin of a blemished animal. Therefore this line of reasoning was faulty. The premise was wrong, so the conclusion was wrong. You cannot use the skin of a blemished animal and you cannot use the skin of a dead animal. Discussions such as these encouraged me that knowing the basic facts in diverse areas of Torah was a necessary prerequisite for proper in-depth learning.

Rabbi Chaim Soloveitchik is quoted as saying, "Anyone who makes novellae without first learning all of *Shas* with *Rashi* is making meaningless novellae." It says in *Berachos* 64a,

"Everyone needs the master of the wheat." *Rashi* explains that everybody needs the one who has wide knowledge of Torah, meaning that you can't grind the wheat until you *have* the wheat. You can't make novellae until you have the facts — but how does one obtain the facts? Obviously I would need a plan.

The bulk of this book is about appropriate long-range financial planning. But there is also planning for long-term spiritual and Torah learning. Money can be budgeted for learning Torah. Time can also be budgeted for learning Torah. It is true that "man proposes and G-d disposes" or "Many are the thoughts of man but the counsel of Hashem — only it will prevail" (*Proverbs* 19:21). In the end it is all in G-d's hands. However, a person can still make reasonable plans. Otherwise, how could we go about our lives?

Stretching out a plan to finish Torah by age 120 is probably not very practical, nor is a plan to finish in just a couple of years. In this day and age I assumed that an average person could expect to live and be relatively healthy at least until age 70, G-d willing. This is also what it says in *Tehillim* (*Psalms* 90:10). I thought that setting a long-term goal to try and become a learned individual sometime between age 60 and 70 was realistic planning, within the realm of what a normal person could hope to accomplish. I was in my early 20s at the time and I thought that I should try to cover as much ground as possible by around age 45. That would hopefully leave me about 25 years or more for solid in-depth learning.

At first glance, learning the entire Torah would seem to be an insurmountable task. "Wisdom is directly in front of an understanding man, but the eyes of a fool are at the end of the earth" (*Proverbs* 17:24). *Rashi* explains that the fool says, "Wisdom is inaccessible to me because it is far from me. How will I be able to learn Tractate *Nezikin,* which consists of 30 chapters (referring to *Bava Kamma, Bava Metzia* and *Bava Basra*); Tractate *Keilim,* consisting of 30 chapters; Tractate *Shabbos,* consisting of 24 chapters." But, for the wise man, it is an easy matter. "Today I will learn two chapters. This is what those who preceded me from time immemorial did." Similarly, "Wisdom is as pearls to the fool; in the gate he will not open his mouth" (*Proverbs* 24:7). *Rashi* explains: .....all wisdom appears to the fool as unattainable as to purchase precious stones and pearls. He says, "How will I learn Torah? When will I attain it?" But the wise man studies a little today and a little tomorrow.

A little today and a little tomorrow, like the drops of water that Rabbi Akiva saw slowly eroding the hard rock.

There are certain obvious plans within Torah learning. The *Chumash* is read each week in the synagogue according to a one-year cycle. Therefore, in my third year of medical school it seemed logical to have a one-year plan to translate every word in the *Chumash* into English and a subsequent one-year plan to learn every *Rashi* in *Chumash* during my senior year. Everyone, of course, knows about the plan to finish *Talmud Bavli* over a seven-and-one-half-year period by learning a *daf* (folio) a day. In reality all areas of Torah can be divided in a similar way. One could look at the *Talmud Yerushalmi* as an insurmountable goal. My particular edition of the *Yerushalmi* has 1554 pages. So I figured I could finish *Yerushalmi* in about four years, at one *daf* a day, or in 1.5 years by learning three *dapim* a day (the basic plan that I followed). *Tosefta* are obscure and difficult, but they are one of the foundations of the Oral Torah. When you look at *Tosefta* as a body of 421 chapters, all of a sudden it does not seem so insurmountable. At a pace of one chapter per day, it would only take 1.2 years to finish. Who could dream of learning the entire *Tur* and the entire four sections of the *Shulchan Aruch*? It certainly seems beyond reach. But the *Tur* and *Shulchan Aruch* have 1704 chapters. They can both be finished in about three years by learning 1.5 chapters a day, or about 10 chapters a week. Other areas of Torah can be similarly broken down into easy-to-manage segments.

First I had to determine what should be included in my plan and then I would have to set reasonable time frames for completing each segment. After much thought, researching what the sources had to say, and speaking to *rabbanim*, I decided that I wanted to learn the following by around age 45:

1.	*Tanach* with commentaries
2.	*Tosefta*
3.	*Mechilta, Sifra, Sifrei*
4.	The Six Orders of the *Mishnah*
5.	*Jerusalem Talmud*
6.	*Babylonian Talmud*
7.	*Mesechtos Ketanos* (printed in standard editions of *Bavli* after *Avodah Zarah*)
8.	*Midrash Rabbah*
9.	*Midrash Tanchuma*
10.	*Tur*
11.	*Shulchan Aruch*

Such a plan would lend itself to automatic review as well. For many years I have tried to learn the entire *Mishnah* yearly. I haven't succeeded in doing it every single year, but in a 17-year period I have managed to finish the entire *Mishnah* about 10 times. That, of course, is review, in and of itself. When I later learn *Tosefta* I am once again reviewing similar material in a different format with some new and different information. Learning *Bavli* and *Yerushalmi* is again a form of review of the same basic material originally laid down in the *Mishnah*. When a topic is finally studied in the *Tur* and *Shulchan Aruch* it will be after having seen the concepts many times, in the *Mishnah,* in the *Tosefta,* in the *Bavli,* and in the *Yerushalmi.* At the very least, the basic concepts, terminology and Talmudic discussions should be familiar. This will then serve as an excellent springboard for subsequent in-depth study of any given area.

Interestingly, I had never put the *Mishneh Torah* of the *Rambam* on my list, even though the *Ramchal* in *Derech Chochmah,* Chapter 5, lists it as a crucial item to learn. There were several reasons for this. Frankly, I didn't think I had the time to learn the *Mishneh Torah* within the framework of my plan. I felt that if there was an opinion of the *Rambam* that was followed as the halachah, then it would be discussed in the *Tur* and *Shulchan Aruch* and in this fashion I would learn the relevant *Rambam*. Of course I was wrong, as I realized before long. It is unthinkable to plan extensive Torah study without the *Rambam*. Upon inquiry I learned that the *Rambam* contains exactly 1,000 chapters. A person could learn three chapters a day for one year or one chapter a day for three years. That certainly seemed manageable to me and in light of an eerie thought I had one day — "How can you die someday without having learned the *Rambam*?" — I decided to add it to my schedule.

At present I am 42, still working on my plan, and still hoping to finish by age 45. With the help of Hashem, so far I have finished:

1. *Mishnayos* about 10 times

2. *Bavli* once with *Rashi*

3. The *Mesechtos Ketanos* once

4. *Mechilta, Sifra, Sifrei* once

5. *Mishneh Torah* and *Sefer HaMitzvos* of the *Rambam* once

6. *Tanach* with commentaries once

7. *Talmud Yerushalmi* once

8. *Tosefta* once

Now I am learning *Midrash Rabbah* (one page a day), *Midrash Tanchuma* (one page a day), and the *Tur* and *Shulchan Aruch* (1.5 chapters per day). I hope to finish these last projects in three to four years, hopefully by age 45.

Then? Then I want to start learning Torah! By that I mean that, having amassed a fund of knowledge, I will be ready to learn in depth, so that I can begin to better understand what I have learned. This is the key to an appreciation of my plan. I have learned large quantities of Torah very quickly. Thanks to my disciplined note-taking and review, I can remember a good deal and can find sources fairly well. I am convinced that when this program is complete, the in-depth portion of my learning career will be very fruitful, because it will build upon a broad fund of knowledge, even though I am the first to admit that, up to now, I have sacrificed depth in favor of breadth.

My wife once pointed to my beautiful large majestic maroon volumes of *Shulchan Aruch* and *Tur* sitting on my study shelf and asked me, "What are those?" I immediately answered, "Those are age 42-45." She meant, "What is in these books? How do they fit into the chain of Oral Law?" But to me, for many years, they have represented what I plan to do with my life from age 42-45. So my automatic response to her was that the *Tur* and *Shulchan Aruch* will be my life from age 42-45. After age 45 my plans are still somewhat nebulous. I would like to spend the rest of my life learning Torah in depth. I still haven't formulated exactly which areas I should try to learn deeply or how to go about it in the proper way. I will seek the advice and guidance of *talmidei chachamim* to try to formulate a reasonable plan sometime in the next three years.

For me this was a 20-25-year plan because I started late and had concurrent responsibilities, such as becoming a doctor and supporting a family. As a late starter, often as a part-timer, I had to follow the path I did. This same path could be followed by other working men who only have a few hours a day to learn. Depending on his schedule and on how much flexibility his primary studies allow him, a yeshivah man, too, could use a few hours of afternoon or night *seder* to learn the breadth of the entire Torah.

Various major areas of Torah can be apportioned to create a disciplined program. Obviously all of these *sefarim* listed below cannot be studied simultaneously; everyone will have to decide for himself how much he can do realistically. Obviously, too, *Talmud Bavli* in the form of *Daf Yomi* should be at the core of every learning program. The fundamentals of Torah could be learned as follows:

1. *Tanach* — 742 chapters — two chapters per day, finish in one year or one chapter per day, finish in two years

2. *Mishnayos* — 523 chapters — 10 chapters per week (1.5 per day), finish every year

3. *Tosefta* — 421 chapters — one chapter per day, finish in just over one year

4. *Talmud Bavli* — Daf Yomi, finish in 7.4 years

5. *Talmud Yerushalmi* — standard editions vary, but mine has 1554 *dapim* — one *daf* per day, finish in just over four years or three *dapim* per day, finish in 1.5 years (basic plan I followed)

6. *Mishneh Torah* — three chapters per day, finish in one year or two chapters per day, finish in 1.5 years;
   one chapter per day, finish in three years

7. *Mesechtos Ketanos* — one *daf* per day, finish in three months

8. *Mechilta, Sifra, Sifrei* — editions vary but can easily be finished in a few months

9. *Midrash Rabbah* and *Tanchuma* — editions vary; my editions are each around 1,000 pages long; learning one page of each per day should enable one to finish in around three years

10. *Tur* and *Shulchan Aruch* — 1,704 chapters — 1.5 simanim per day or ten per week enables one to finish in around three years

Even if none of these projects overlapped, the total would take just 20 years. But, depending on one's personal schedule and inclination, one could undertake more than one program a day. There are many variations depending on one's skills, available time, and interests.

A. SAMPLE 20-YEAR PLAN TO FINISH THE ENTIRE TORAH

a. Two chapters of *Tanach* per day for one year, then

b. 10 chapters of *Mishnah* per week for one year (repeat *Mishnah* yearly) then

c. one chapter of *Tosefta* per day for 1.2 years,

d. one *daf Bavli* per day for 7.4 years,

e. one *daf Yerushalmi* per day for 4.3 years,

f. three chapters of *Mishneh Torah* per day for one year,

g. 1.5 chapters of *Tur* and *Shulchan Aruch* per day for 3.1 years

h. two pages of *Midrash Rabbah* and *Midrash Tanchuma* per day for 1.5 years

i. learn the *Mesechtos Ketanos* and *Mechilta, Sifra, Sifrei* when you can (finishing each in a few months)

TOTAL TIME SPENT LEARNING THE ENTIRE PROJECT — 20 YEARS

Many of the above projects could be overlapped and doubled up by someone who is spending his entire day learning Torah. Even as a working man I have managed to double up many of these projects over the years. A sample program could be as follows *Talmud Bavli* should again be at its core throughout:

B. SAMPLE 10-YEAR PLAN TO FINISH THE ENTIRE TORAH

a. Two chapters *Tanach* per day and 1.5 chapters *Mishnah* per day and one chapter *Tosefta* per day (coordinate with *Mishnah*) for one year (review *Mishnah* yearly), then,

b. two *daf Bavli* and one *daf Yerushalmi* per day for four years

c. three chapters *Mishneh Torah* per day and three pages *Midrash* per day for one year

d. 1.5 chapters of *Tur* and *Shulchan Aruch* per day for three years

e. learn the *mesechtos ketanos* and *Mechilta, Sifra, Sifrei* when you can (finishing each in a few months)

TOTAL TIME TO FINISH THE ENTIRE PROJECT — 10 YEARS!

A person should not get discouraged that by sticking to a broad-based learning program he will acquire only superficial knowledge. Remember, it is only the first time through. The *Chasam Sofer* is quoted as telling his son, the *K'sav Sofer*, that the first time through *Shas* he should skip all the second opinions ("*lishna acharina*") in *Rashi*. How much can a person understand and retain by learning such vast amounts and so quickly his first time through? It's all relative. I would hope that I know more than I knew 20 years ago; certainly I know less than I want to know 20 years from now. I am not expecting to be a learned man the first time through. My goal is to be a learned man when I am 70. At present there are some parts of Torah that I understand well, some parts that I do not understand at all, and some parts that I understand on an average level.

As a very helpful study and memory aid, I keep a vast amount of notes, mostly in English, summarizing *sugyos* in both *Talmuds*, chapters of *Mishnah*, chapters of *Tanach*, etc. I have one loose-leaf binder with the *Tanach* summarized in English, one for the *Mishnah*, one for the *Tosefta*, four binders for *Talmud Bavli*, and four binders for *Talmud Yerushalmi*. These are not *chiddushim* (novellae), just basic summaries, cross references, and other useful study aids. With the aid of my review program and voluminous summary notes in English, I can often find the facts I need at least to discuss a topic intelligently with my family or friends. Please see Appendix 6 for my article on the value of taking notes to help Torah learning, entitled *Please, Take Note*, which appeared in *The Jewish Observer*, March 1985.

For example, my 11-year-old son Moishe and my 9-year-old son Chaim Mordechai recently told me that they had learned in *cheder* that Esau would shoot arrows with such accuracy that he could *shecht* (ritually slaughter) flying birds in midair. Moishe and Chaim Mordechai asked me if that would really be a kosher *shechitah*. I didn't know offhand, but I did remember once having seen a relevant discussion in Tractate *Chullin*. I thought it was in the first two chapters. Reviewing two chapters of *Chullin* would take me all day, and I would probably never find what I needed. So I went to my English notes, and in less than five minutes found that the discussion was on *daf* 31b,32a. Then we looked it up in the tractate and an interesting discussion ensued. This type of thing happens all the time in my home and at my Shabbos table. We can usually have lively and fairly intelligent discussions of areas of interest, once we locate the relevant Talmudic sources.

A similar example recently occurred. I was learning Tractate *Ma'aser Sheni* in the *Yerushalmi* and came across a discussion in Chapter 1, Halachah 1, which stated that it is forbidden to betroth a woman with fruit from the Sabbatical year. I remembered learning over 10 years ago in Tractate *Kiddushin* in the *Bavli* that you *can* betroth a woman with such fruit. The contradiction bothered me, but I really could not remember where in *Kiddushin* I had seen the *sugya*. To review all of *Kiddushin* inside would not be practical, and would take hours or days. My English notes summarizing *Talmud Bavli* came to the rescue. I was able to locate the relevant *sugya* in a matter of minutes and look it up (52a). Much to my delight, *Tosafos* there answered my question.

Just last night as I was finishing this chapter, my father-in-law and I got into a discussion of the heights of domains, pertaining to the halachos of Shabbos. I told him that I had once learned that a private domain extends all the way up to the sky, as opposed to a public domain which extends only for 10 handbreadths. He asked me where I had seen that. I knew it was somewhere in the first chapter of Tractate *Shabbos*, but I had no idea where. I used my English summary notes, and within a minute I found the reference on 7a-b. Then we were able to study the *Gemara* and pursue our discussion further.

When learning the breadth of Torah, there will obviously be times when the material is exceedingly difficult. While learning *Yerushalmi* I sometimes cannot fathom even the simple meaning of a *sugya*, even after reading the classic commentaries *Korban HaEidah* and *P'nei Moshe*, or the newer commentary of R' Chaim Kanievsky. There are many overlapping and often contradictory textual emendations in the *Tosefta*. This often makes it difficult for me to read the *Tosefta* through smoothly and fully understand its meaning. Still, that need not be a deterrent for learning these areas the first time through.

On the verse "And it will come to pass if you shall hearken diligently..." (*Deut.* 28:1), *Midrash Tanchuma* comments that if you have learned something in this world, then you can learn it in the World to Come, but if you didn't learn it in this world you cannot learn it in the World to Come. Similarly the *Tz'lach* on *Berachos* says "Learn Aggadah and things you don't understand to be prepared to learn and delight in the Torah in the World to Come. Just as a child learns *Aleph Beis* and doesn't understand and it seems like a waste to him, he subsequently sees its value, when he reads and comprehends."

The *Chafetz Chaim* says (*Shem Olam, Shaar Hahis'chazkus,* end of Chapter 4): "All of the Torah that one has learned in this world will be comprehended in depth in the next world. However, if one has not studied a particular tractate from *Shas*, he will then, Heaven forbid, lack this particular knowledge forever." Rabbi Yisrael Zev Gustman, when he was a 10-year-old boy, was told by the *Chafetz Chaim* to learn something difficult, even if he did not understand it. The *Chafetz Chaim* explained that when the soul will be removed from the body in the World to Come, it will come out with full understanding of what was learned, even if it had been unclear during life. It is like a cataract that blocks light from entering the eye; the visual abilities of the retina and eye behind the cataract are inherently healthy. But this will apply only if the material was learned at least once on earth.

The *Chafetz Chaim* rejoiced when he heard Rabbi Meir Shapiro's idea for *Daf Yomi*, the worldwide study of a folio page of the Talmud every day. The *Chafetz Chaim* said that now everyone will learn all of *Shas*, even neglected *mesechtos* such as *Nazir*. Those classrooms had been sitting empty in the World to Come. Now that people would learn these volumes in this world, even on a superficial level, they would be eligible to attend the classes on *Nazir* in the World to Come. When Rabbi Elchonon Wasserman heard these words from the *Chafetz Chaim*, he started crying. The one *mesechta* he had never learned up to that time was *Nazir*!

There is another remarkable and wonderful advantage to a *bikiyus* program. It can help you to increase your total learning time. How? It is very hard to learn a *Tosafos* or a *Rabbi Akiva Eiger* while waiting on line in the bank, or sitting on a train, or in the few minutes a physician may have between reading x-rays. But *bikiyus* lends itself to filling up these empty spaces. Such spaces are perfect for a *Mishnah*, or a *Tosefta,* or a few verses from *Nach*. They are even perfect for glancing at a page of *Yerushalmi* to start getting the flow of the *sugya* or a chapter of *Mishneh Torah*. Total learning time during the day can be increased dramatically. This, of course, is in addition to regular fixed learning periods.

Talmud Bavli can be learned not only in the *beis midrash,* but also on lines at Israeli banks, on lines in Albany supermarkets, in emergency rooms between x-rays, and in countless other places. When I finally approached the end of Tractate *Niddah* in Baltimore in 1989, the last page of *Talmud Bavli,* I wanted to learn it in a holy place, so I decided to finish the last *daf* in the *beis midrash* of Yeshivah Ner Israel. On the momentous day, I went to do some errands before continuing to the yeshivah. Among other stops I went to the Baltimore Public Library to quickly look up something in the latest issue of *Money* magazine. Someone else was reading the issue I needed so I patiently sat down to wait. Of course, I took out my *Bavli* and started learning. I was sitting there longer than expected. I did not want to stop learning, so much to my surprise, and chagrin, I actually finished *Talmud Bavli* in the public library, of all places.

For years this sort of upset me. I had wanted to learn the last *daf* in a holy place, a memorable place, like a *beis midrash*. I was crestfallen that my momentous completion of *Bavli* occurred in a public library. Maybe Hashem would think poorly of me for having stopped off to check a financial magazine. A few years ago I was reading Magnetic Resonance Imaging exams (MRI's) in an imaging center where an observant lawyer worked. She noticed that I always learned *Yerushalmi* between MRI scans. We got to talking and I mentioned how I had finished *Bavli* in the public library and how that had always bothered me. She said, "It is the opposite. Think of how wonderful that is. You showed Hashem that wherever you are, instead of wasting time you learn Torah. Anybody can finish *Shas Bavli* in a *beis midrash.* But it is extra special that you finished in the public library waiting to read a magazine!" I had never thought of it that way before. That really cheered me up.

We are very fortunate to live in an age where so many Torah works are available to the public, such as *Tosefta* with commentary *Chazon Yechezkal,* the *Sifra* with commentary of the *Chafetz Chaim,* new editions of *Mesechta Kallah* and countless other works, such as the ArtScroll Series and the Schottenstein Talmud in English and Hebrew. A few years ago I came across two halachos in *Mishneh Torah,* concerning monetary laws, but containing side points germane to this idea.

The first is in *Hilchos Malveh v'Loveh* (15:2), which discusses the law pertaining to payment of a loan when the lender had insisted on being paid back in front of witnesses. The borrower claims that his payment was indeed witnessed, but that the witnesses had traveled to another country. *Rambam* rules that the borrower is believed. He says that those who rule otherwise base themselves on erroneous versions of the *Gemara.* *Rambam* continues — "... in Egypt there came into my hands a piece of an old *Gemara* written on parchment, which they wrote on about 500 years ago. I found two versions and both say if the borrower claims he paid in front of two witnesses and they have gone to another country that he is believed ..."

The second *Rambam* is in *Hilchos Eidus* (12:1), where he rules that someone who commits a sin is not a halachically acceptable witness. *Rambam* explains that this applies to a sin that everyone would know not to do, such as swearing falsely, stealing, etc. But if it is a sin that most people are not aware of, then the person is still kosher to a be witness. He continues, "... for example, they saw him tying or untying on Shabbos. They need to let him know that this is desecrating Shabbos because the majority of the people do not know this ..."

Think how amazing these two statements are. Before the invention of the printing press, the *Rambam* had to learn from handwritten *Gemaras* and other source material. But there were times he even had to search through old *genizos* in Egypt to find 500 year old torn scraps of parchment in order to determine the proper wording of the *Talmud*. And there was such a dearth of manuscripts for the general populace that the majority did not even know that tying knots on Shabbos is forbidden. Today even the most recent *ba'al teshuvah* learns quickly that you may not tie knots on Shabbos. Today we have an overflowing abundance of English and Hebrew books to help even the novice learn *davening, kashrus,* Shabbos, the holidays, etc.

About a year ago my wife and I spent a week in Philadelphia, while I attended a medical conference at the University of Pennsylvania. One afternoon we took a walk downtown by the Liberty Bell, and happened to walk by the old Benjamin Franklin printing shop. A National Park Ranger was demonstrating how the Declaration of Independence was printed over 200 years ago using an old-fashioned printing press. It was fascinating to see her set the individual letters by hand in the wooden frame. Then she spread thick black ink on the letters with a special sponge. Finally she manually laid a parchment over the letters and cranked the press down by hand. Each page was hung up to dry individually.

I thought of the standard pages found in our *Talmuds* and *Shulchan Aruchs*, with their complicated layouts containing all the side commentaries. It must have been unbelievably difficult to have typeset these pages by hand, one by one. Each folio was individually printed and hung up to dry, one by one. Because of this hard work by unknown workers over a century ago, we are blessed today with such beautifully laid-out pages. Most modern printings of our classic books today utilize photo-offset reproductions of the originally laid out pages from long ago, because it would be so hard to duplicate the original layouts from scratch.

We are so blessed today! We have such beautifully printed *Gemaras* and *Mishnayos.* Our *Yerushalmis* and *Toseftos* are wonderful and so easy to learn from. What used to be obscure material is now so readily available. There are beautiful versions of *Sifra* or *Mesechta Kallah.* The *Chafetz Chaim* writes in his introduction to his commentary on the *Sifra* that he came across what was the only handwritten version of the emendations of the *Gra* on *Sifra* and begged the owner to let him borrow it and reprint it. Today I learn *Sifra* with the very version that the *Chafetz Chaim* published. It is beautifully printed and so easy on the eye to read. Yet, just 75 years ago, only one copy existed, and it was handwritten. That would have been impossible for me to learn. Today we are fortunate to have at our fingertips a world of Torah that even a short time ago was so hard to access.

We should be so grateful to Hashem. We live in an age when wisdom is literally running in the streets crying out to us to be learned, to be read cover to cover. I am so grateful every day to Hashem for the miracle of having so many important sources of Torah available to me in such beautiful volumes, in such eye-pleasing format. We should rejoice at the bountiful heavenly blessings of this period. The best way to show gratitude to the Creator for His kindness is by acquiring these books and by learning them cover to cover.

To this day do you know what gives me my greatest feeling of pride in my learning? My study at home is filled with *sefarim*, like many other homes. In many homes you can find volumes of *Mishnah* or *Chumash* or a *siddur* that are cracked from overuse. My volumes of *Talmud Yerushalmi* sit on one shelf. The bindings of several volumes are cracked and discolored from use. Whenever I pass my *Yerushalmi* and see the cracked bindings I get a tremendous feeling of pride and accomplishment.

G–d willing all of our homes should have worn-out *Yerushalmis*!

5

STOCKS VS. THE STOCK MARKET

My wife and I started on our goal of early retirement by being frugal. There wasn't too much else we could do as I was putting in endless hours in a radiology residency and was only making about $20,000 a year. My wife taught occasionally and that brought in a few thousand more. Our rent in those days was only $250 for a three-bedroom flat. We had only one child and he was not in school yet. In those three years of my final medical training we managed to save around $10,000. This was 1982-1985.

After finishing my radiology training in 1985 I went on to do part-time medical work for about four years. I would work intermittently and spend the rest of the time learning Torah. People think that "temp" jobs are only available for secretaries and the like, but there is actually a thriving market for temps in the professions such as medicine, law, accounting, etc. A medical practice may need someone to fill in for a partner who is on a lengthy vacation. Or perhaps a partner had retired and they needed temporary help until they hired someone else. Once I even subbed for a practice where a physician had suddenly died of a heart attack in his prime! What a forceful lesson to bring home what it says in *Mishnah Avos*, "If not now, when?" (1:14) as well as "Repent one day before your death" (2:10). This made me even more determined to try to start learning Torah full time as soon as I could.

These temporary jobs were actually pretty interesting. I was able to travel to different parts of the country. I practiced radiology in a hospital on an Indian reservation in upstate New York and I read x-rays at Tuskegee Institute in Alabama, founded by Dr. George Washington Carver over 100 years ago. I had to turn down a few jobs in more exotic locales such as Hawaii or an island off the coast of Alaska, for the simple reason that I would not be able to get kosher food in those locations. I once had a temporary job in Lancaster, Pennsylvania and with my beard everyone assumed I was Amish.

Temporary positions usually pay well as the people are somewhat desperate, and they don't have to provide benefits such as health insurance or pension. Most of my jobs were arranged through a medical temp agency, CompHealth, that operates out of Salt Lake City and Atlanta. CompHealth would pay me a daily rate and also supply a plane ticket to the job , a hotel room, and malpractice insurance. Some jobs I arranged on my own through a network of colleagues, but then I was on my own for all expenses.

During these years (1985-1989) I never worked more than half a year and usually earned between $30,000 and $80,000 a year. During this period we lived a good deal of the time in *Eretz Yisrael*, where living expenses were less than in the U.S. During these four years our savings and investments continued to steadily accumulate. Our funds were invested almost exclusively in bonds, mostly purchased with the help of a broker friend of mine in Chicago, who specializes in bonds.

At this point (1990) I entered a partnership track in a Baltimore radiology practice and was a senior partner by 1992. From May 1990 until May 1996 when I retired, I was worked intensely full time. I still learned Torah, but not as much as in prior years. These were the only years when I truly made "doctors' money." At this point I was at a real crossroads. If the gravy train would last, and if I so desired, then I could lead the luxurious life with a big house and continually new and expensive cars. Or I could take the path less traveled. I took the path which led to a simple three-bedroom house in a working-class neighborhood with a Ford and Chrysler in the driveway (no garage).

Firstly and practically, I really didn't think that the gravy train would last. Even in 1990 the winds of managed care, HMO's, Medicare and Medicaid cutbacks, crises in malpractice and other issues were already blowing faintly and getting a lot stronger. More importantly, I really didn't want to waste the significant income I was about to receive on luxuries. I really wanted to retire at age 40 and learn Torah. And if I did choose to do further work in medicine, I wanted it to be for idealistic reasons, not just for the money. In fact, in my semiretirement, when I do medical work, I enjoy it more than I ever did.

After giving my situation some serious thought, I realized I would have to invest the anticipated money in vehicles that would grow, that could carry me through an early retirement, yet would be reasonably safe. What an education I needed. All during my growing-up years and medical school years I did nothing but singlemindedly pursue my studies and medical research. I was accepted to medical school at 16 and entered at 18. I was dissecting bodies in the morgue and blasting off blood tests into space in high school. But money? Investments? I hadn't a clue. When I first married I didn't know how to balance a checkbook nor how to buy a CD (Certificate of Deposit — not compact disc). I knew that to realize my goals I would need stocks.

I was scared. I thought the stock market was dangerous and rigged. By this time the 1987 crash had already occurred (but for that matter so had the astonishing subsequent rebound). At this point though, I thought that stocks and the stock market were synonymous. I read books in the library, written by Benjamin Graham, Charles Schwab, Peter Lynch and others, on how to invest in stocks. I read what others wrote about Warren Buffet's methods. I learned quite a few things.

First and foremost I learned that the stock market is indeed crazy, but stocks are not crazy. And the stock market is not the same thing as stocks. When you own a good stock that you have researched and understand, you actually own a small piece of a good business. Owning a small piece of General Electric, if you understand the company, is like owning a neighborhood business where you know the market, the neighborhood, the competition, and what your customers need. When a local business owner understands the business he is in, serves a need, is good to his customers, is honest, and makes a steady profit, then he will have a growing business. In fact, my medical practice was a small business run by six of us.

My little piece of multibillion-dollar GE or 3M is the same thing. If a large corporation is good to its customers, gives good service, knows its business, competes honestly and ethically, is innovative and adaptive, then it will thrive. The business will grow, the earnings will grow, and eventually the stock price will grow to reflect that. But in the short term? That is where the craziness of the stock market comes in. If there is a sudden war somewhere and the stock market goes down, does that have anything at all to do with the intrinsic value of GE or 3M or American Water Works or Tampa Electric? Of course not. The stock market's fluctuations in the short term are for the most part totally crazy and irrational.

Any of the stocks I have bought could crash tomorrow if the market crashes. But I believe that none of my companies will be less effective companies tomorrow or in 5 years or in 10 years. In fact I firmly believe that all of my companies are well positioned for decades of growth. And I truly believe that in 20-30 years my stocks will have gone up handsomely to reflect this growth. I always tell people, "Look, I have good stocks. But if you buy any one of them, it could drop 50 percent tomorrow. I can never predict or anticipate the tomorrow of the stock market. But, if you hold these stocks for 10 or 20 or 30 years you will be very handsomely rewarded." I sincerely believe that to be so. After all, I have put my money where my mouth is.

Of course some aspects of stock prices are rational. If there is a major oil embargo, then an oil-burning utility could drop in price for good reasons. If a company gets embroiled in a major liability suit with threat of a crippling judgment, then the price of that company may logically go down. This is where proper diversification comes in and I will discuss that later. The market irrational when the prices of all stocks go up or down for no good fundamental reason.

Even with this irrationality of the stock market in the short term, there is one rational thing that will always win out. That is, over long periods of time a stock's price will closely track its earnings. If a company constantly earns ever increasing amounts of money, then in the long term its price will appreciate accordingly. There may be irrational ups and downs like the shape of a sine curve between point A today and point B which is 20-30 years hence. But, for a good company, point B will always be well above point A.

I learned several other important fundamental principles of successful stock investing. Buy individual stocks and not mutual funds. Buy stocks that have paid rising dividends for endless decades.

6

MORE THOUGHTS ON STOCK MARKET RISK

Dr. Jeremy Siegel, in Chapter 30 of his book *Stocks for the Long Run*, summarizes data on the history of every stock listed on the New York Stock Exchange over a 65-year period, from 1926 to 1991. The data was originally compiled by the Center for Research in Security Prices in Chicago. This is the most comprehensive and authoritative study of the U.S. stock market ever performed. It took five years to compile by computer. Basically, from 1926 through 1991 there are 2211 possible year-to-year combinations (e.g. — 1926-1927, 1926-1928, 1926-1929, 1927-1928, 1927-1929, etc.).

Studying all of these 2211 combinations, only 72 periods show a loss. This is only 3 percent of the time. During the other 97 percent of the time an individual would have made money in stocks. If a person held onto his stocks for at least 7 years, there were only five times when he would have lost money from 1926-1991. If a person held onto his stocks for 10 years or more, he would NEVER have lost money between 1926 and 1991. That is to say, during the entire 65 years from 1926 to 1991, stocks have never lost money when held for 10 years or more. And this includes the great depression of the 1930s as well as the terrible bear market of the early 1970s. These statistics assume that all dividends were reinvested. You will learn in Chapter 6 of this book why that is so important.

Stocks can and will go down. Drops of 20-30 percent are relatively common and drops of 50 percent or more are not unheard of. This can be catastrophic for a short-term investor. But as a long-term investor this works to your advantage. How? If you are steadily putting away $10 a week into a stock such as Coca Cola and a share of Coke is selling for $20, then you can buy a half share each week. If the price were to crash to $10 then you are fortunate enough to be able to buy a full share each week. That extra half share per week really adds up over the years. When the stock price eventually goes back up, the shares you bought cheaply will give you your highest profits. If you are constantly investing small amounts week after week, then the market dips give you opportunities to buy shares on sale. It's like getting 50 percent off the price of your groceries, week after week. As the investment guru Philip Fischer said, "It's like buying dollar bills for 50 cents each."

In short, never, ever invest in stocks if you may need the money in five years or less. If you can leave the money untouched for between five and ten years, your risk drops dramatically. Once you can put the money away for 10 years, or more, then stocks become a very safe way to invest, your chances of losing money are virtually nil, and you will get more growth than any other investment vehicle can provide.

Let us look at some practical examples. If a person were unlucky enough to buy stocks the day before the great stock-market crash of 1929, he would have lost, on paper, 38 percent of his money by the next year. That would only be a real loss if he panicked and sold out at the bottom. But if he held onto his stocks until 1939, then he would already have an annualized profit of 7.76 percent. Not great, but not a disaster. By holding on until 1945 the annualized profit would have grown to 14.74 percent per year — a fantastic return! If he continued to hold until 1959, a 30-year period, the annual return would by 14.09 percent — doubling his money every five years for 30 years! This assumes a one-time investment right before the great stock-market crash of 1929. If a person were to have faithfully invested $10 per week during this entire time, then the return would be astronomically higher, because all along he would be picking up shares cheaply.

Let us look at a more recent example, the great bear market of the early 1970s. If a person bought stocks in 1972, right before the terrible bear market, by 1973 he would have lost 29 percent of his funds and he would have lost an additional 28 percent in 1974. That is a loss of 57 percent in just two years! But if the person would patiently have held on until 1982, then his annualized profit would turn out be 14 percent, which doubles the money every five years. By 1991 the annualized profit would be 13.58 percent per year. Again, this assumes reinvestment of all dividends. Once again, if he had invested additional amounts weekly during the bad times, then the eventual profits would be much higher.

Let us assume you follow my advice and patiently let your money ride through the bad years. What if the market crashes just when you were about to finally cash in? While it may be unpleasant to see your stocks go down the day before you sell them, if you have already held them for long enough, the remaining profits will still be very great. Let us take some practical examples.

A family puts $100 into Coca Cola stock for a newborn baby girl and adds $10 a week for 20 years. The result is $68,000 by age 20, just in time to make a wedding and help support a son-in-law in *kollel*. If the market were to crash by 50 percent there would be only $34,000 left. It would be very sad to have lost half your profits. But if the money had been in a bank savings account during those 20 years earning 2 percent per year it would have only grown to $13,000. If the bank had paid 5 percent they would have $18,000. So, even in the unlikely event of a 50 percent market crash, the family is still way ahead with stocks. If they can pay for the wedding, etc. with other funds, then chances are their stocks will bounce back in a few years. Remember the example above for 1973 and 1974 when stocks went down a total of 57 percent? In 1975 the stock market went back up 62 percent! There is no guarantee, but usually waiting a few extra years will erase your losses.

Over longer periods of time, the problems due to a market crash are even less of a problem. Let us say a *bar-mitzvah* boy puts away $100 in Coca Cola stock at age 13 and adds $10 per week for 47 years. At age 60 he would have $4 million. If the market were to crash 50 percent just before his retirement, he would still have $2 million. Nothing to sneeze at. And why would he have to cash it all in at once and take the loss? Let him cash in what he needs to live on for a few years and leave the rest intact to await the eventual market rebound. Even if he decided to sell all at once, he still has $2 million. If he had put the money in the bank for 47 years at 2 percent he would only have $41,000. That's correct, $41,000 versus $2 million. If the bank had paid him 5 percent per year he would still only have $99,500. No question about it. Patiently stick with stocks for the long term.

7

INDIVIDUAL STOCKS VS. MUTUAL FUNDS

My research taught me another fundamental truth. Individual stocks are better than most mutual funds for most people. Individual people who research good stocks carefully, and are patient, can beat the so-called professionals almost anytime. This is not just a doctor's ego talking. Remember, I told you before that most doctors make lousy investors and money managers. This is not my ego talking. This is common sense talking.

First and foremost, nobody and no one cares more about my own money than I do. And no one in the world will ever care more about your own money than you will. That alone should make us the better guardians of our nest eggs than any professional could ever be. Professional mutual fund managers have many agendas, besides just making your nest egg grow. They have to answer to committees for every investment they make. They will therefore buy IBM even if it is not a good stock as opposed to Dover Corporation which may be an excellent stock. As they say, no one ever lost their job by buying IBM. They must pick the presently popular investments to keep their jobs. Well, you say, aren't there contrarian funds — which specifically target unpopular, rejected stocks? All I know is that Fidelity Contrafund, during the brief period I owned it, often had large positions in traditional stocks such as Microsoft, Disney, Pepsi-Co, Gillette and Cisco which are not contrarian stocks by any means.

Which brings me to a second point. Mutual funds are often outright misleading. A fund labeled as contrarian may have all sorts of noncontrarian stocks in it. Fidelity Blue Chip Stock fund is another good example. Blue chip invokes images of GE, 3M and other industrial stalwarts in my mind and the mind of any reasonable investor. But the Blue Chip Stock fund invested mainly in FUTURE blue chips. Which means high-flying technology start-ups, biotech start-ups, IPO's, and other decidedly nonblue chip companies. Speak of misleading.

I also briefly owned Fidelity Asset Manager. This fund was supposed to scientifically balance cash, bonds, and stocks to achieve decent, conservative, steady growth in any market environment without the risks associated with more growth-oriented mutual funds. Instead, it took a whopping multibillion-dollar gamble on Mexican and Latin American bonds and lost big time. I lost money and so did many others. Scientific? Right! The investment did not at all reflect the proposed methodology of the fund. If I was this scientific in my medical practice then I would be brought up on malpractice charges.

Why did these fund managers do this? Because each one wanted to beat the averages and beat each other. They were concerned about their year-end bonus which depends on absolute performance and relative performance against the indexes and their peers. They were most decidedly not primarily concerned only with the long-term growth of my nest egg. I am obviously not the only one aware of this. Major mutual fund companies have made massive shake-ups recently, and are trying to get managers to be true to their stated objectives. Many managers have left or been pushed out. But it is a bit contradictory. On the one hand the funds claim that they want their fund managers to abide by the stated fund objectives, but on the other hand they will push a manager out or lower his bonus if he doesn't perform stupendously in relationship to his peers. That tends to lead a manager to go out on a limb and take high-flying chances with my money. Speak of mixed messages.

Besides, what exactly is a fund? What is the Magellan fund? It is an ever changing collection of stocks, often being bought by a new person, with new and increasing amounts of money to invest. The name Magellan may stay the same but there is no way on earth that Magellan today has any resemblance at all to Peter Lynch's Magellan. First of all, the stocks within it are totally different. Secondly, with less than a few billion dollars to invest, Mr. Lynch was able to make a winner really pay off as a significant percentage of the whole portfolio. And he could invest in smaller companies. Today, with over $50 billion to invest, no single winner can make much difference to the whole fund. And with so much new money coming in, the fund can no longer easily invest in fast-growing small companies. Most importantly, Peter Lynch is gone (he retired young to spend more time with his family).[1] How can a basket of different stocks, with a different manager, with a different amount of cash to invest be considered the same thing it was 10 years ago? The name is the same, but the fund is absolutely not the same.

But GE? Or 3M? Or Duke Power? Or Wachovia Bank? These are among my stocks. Unless GE sells all its factories and goes into making ketchup it is more or less the same GE it has always been. Hewlett Packard and Gillette pretty much stay the same over the years unless HP decides to do something crazy like make hamburgers and Gillette starts to sell automobiles. Of course companies do change. But not that much. Their size can change. The manager can change. The inventions can

---

1. His replacement, Morris Smith, was an observant Jew who left the helm of the Magellan fund after a brief period and went to learn in *Eretz Yisrael*.

change and the products can change. But, more or less, my Coke, my Gillette, my Tampa Electric, and my Bristol Myer Squibb are the same ones my grandfather could have bought in the early 1900s.

When December rolls around, mutual fund managers will often sell stocks that have under-performed during the preceding year. They do not have the patience or ability to let a good investment come into its own over time. Why? Because in December the fund has to publish an annual report. They have to have good year-end figures and publish a list of what they own. They want the fund holders to see good stuff on the list, even if it has been on the list only a week. They don't want any losers, even if the loser had good long-term potential.

This year-end selling affects your nest egg's performance negatively in several ways. First of all, a good but lagging stock is not given time to come into its own. A good stock that may have temporarily dropped in price will not be purchased at a bargain rate. It will be passed over to put a winner in the portfolio to dress up the year-end list. In a nonpension account, this December selling generates taxable capital gains for you.

But as an individual I bought Cincinnati Bell Telephone in small blocks over a five-year period. I knew it was an excellent stock with good long-term potential. (see graph on Cincinnati Bell purchases in Chapter 12). And for five years it did nothing. I kept buying in at a price range of 8-8.5. Then it finally bloomed, as I knew it would, and it shot up to over 30. It took me five years of patient waiting. Because I kept buying in on the cheap, this became one of my best stocks. Conversely, I also kept buying General Electric in small blocks over the years (see graph on GE purchases in Chapter 12). GE just kept going up and up, and each subsequent purchase came in at a higher price. So over all, my steady growing GE has not done as well as my late-blooming Cincinnati Bell.

I have also had the nerve to buy a good stock when it is going down. I can have the ability to buy a stock as the price sinks because I have no fund holders or managers to answer to each December (only my wife). I know my stocks are good, and the lower price gives me a chance to buy them on sale. So I kept on buying Eli Lilly and Company as it went from 21.5 to 11.5 (see graph, Chapter 12). And I kept on buying Boeing as it went from 30 to 17.5 (see graph, Chapter 12). Now Lilly is 80 and Boeing is 52.5. The shares I bought as they went down in price were among my best performers when the stocks finally rebounded.

I had the confidence to buy stocks that went nowhere for years or stocks that went down for years because I had thoroughly researched them and knew them to be good companies with long-term potential. Of course some stocks go nowhere or go down because they have real fundamental problems in their own company or in their peer industry as a whole. Buggy whips in the 1920s were not good stocks to buy as they were going down. They obviously went down for the final count, and for good reason.

And then there are the fees. Mutual funds often charge a load or commission to get in. Right up front you may give away 3 — 5 percent of your money. Then there are the yearly fees which can average 1.5 percent — 2 percent a year or more. Year after year these fees are eating away at the growth of your capital. When you buy mutual funds through a supermarket one-stop shop like Charles Schwab One Stop or Fidelity's Fund Supermarket, another quarter percent or so is tacked on each year for the convenience of one-stop shopping between fund families; thousands more of your dollars down the drain.

With my portfolio of 22 stocks, my only cost has been purchase commissions. I mostly used a discount broker and the total cost to amass my stocks over a seven-year period has come to less than 2 percent of the portfolio's value. And that's it. No more fees for life. I pay nothing to maintain the accounts and my dividends reinvest for free. If I had hundreds of thousands of dollars in a mutual fund which clipped me an average yearly fee of 1.5 percent I would be paying thousands of dollars just to hold the account. In my own portfolio, those thousands go back to work for me for free. And over decades I expect those thousands to add up big time.

I will end this chapter with a small exception to my rule. I dabbled in a few Fidelity and Scudder funds years ago until I wised up. But even today I hold two mutual funds and add to them regularly; $100 monthly transferred electronically from my checking account to each fund. They are index funds. They offer a safe, easy way to add small amounts to the market via dollar-cost averaging. And they have virtually none of the negatives of other mutual funds. Fees are minimal as index funds do very little trading. Taxes are minimal for the same reason. As the funds get bigger and bigger, performance is not affected. After all, they buy the large index, not some small start-up companies. And if the manager changes, who cares? The manager of Vanguard's Index 500 fund goes each day to one old computer and puts in a disc which captures the amount of new money that has come in. He then goes to a second computer, inserts the disc, and the computer automatically invests the new money to match the index. That is the total extent of active management. If the manager changes I believe my fund is still safe!

I own the Vanguard Index 500 fund which tracks the S&P 500 and only charges a minuscule 0.19 percent a year in fees (which is usually covered by the dividends paid out). My second index fund is the TIAA Stock Index Fund. It tracks the Russell 3000 by holding around 1100 representative stocks from that larger index. The S&P 500 covers about 70 percent over U.S. equities and the Russell 3000 covers 98 percent. So the second index fund gives me some coverage of smaller companies. The fee is a low 0.4 percent a year.

However, it is not available to the general public. TIAA stands for Teachers Insurance and Annuity Association. It is a group set up almost 100 years ago by Andrew Carnegie to offer low-cost insurance and annuities to those involved in education. I taught at The University of Maryland Medical School so I qualified. My father sold Prudential insurance for years. He told me that even if he gave me his entire commission as a gift, he still couldn't beat TIAA's prices.[1] TIAA is rated

---

1. This is not a book about insurance, but if you work in a hospital or school (day schools and *kollel* may count as well) and you want life insurance, you will find no product in the country priced lower than TIAA's insurance offerings. My wife and I both have TIAA policies.

A plus by all four insurance-rating agencies. It is virtually unmatched in the industry. Its flagship fund is the TIAA-CREF (college retirement equity fund) which has returned 15 percent on average since the 1950s. This fund is larger than Magellan but since it is not offered to the general public the media always calls Magellan the largest fund in the country.

If you are a teacher or hospital worker, then grab one of TIAA's offerings. Day school teachers and *kollel* members may very well be eligible as well. If not, there are many index funds at Vanguard covering the S&P 500, small cap stocks, foreign stocks, and more.

Now, for the most important fundamental truth to profitable long-term investing:

DIVIDENDS! DIVIDENDS! DIVIDENDS!

8

DIVIDENDS

A h, dividends! I enjoy my Talmudic studies. I enjoy my
family. I enjoy the little medicine which I still practice.
And I confess I also enjoy checking the newspaper
each morning to see if any of my stocks have raised
their dividends. Watching the stalwarts of American industry
which I own regularly paying and raising their dividends is one
of my small pleasures. I recently began following my stocks
through a customized portfolio newsletter from Reuter's which I
designed for myself using computer programs. Now I can find
out about my dividend increases the night before and don't
have to wait for the morning paper. Progress!

Already these dividend increases and reinvestments have
raised the yield on my original investment from 3.02 percent to
4.7 percent in just 8 years (see bar graph on p. 86). By age 60
my dividend yield may actually grow enough to support us on income alone. *Money Magazine* in January 1996 detailed the
investing story of Anne Scheiber, the woman who turned $5000

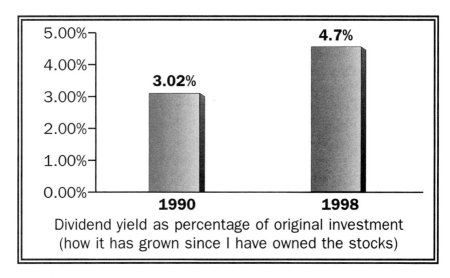

Dividend yield as percentage of original investment
(how it has grown since I have owned the stocks)

into $22 million through careful long-term stock investing. By the time of her death at age 101 her dividends alone were coming in at about $750,000 a year. She left her entire fortune to Yeshiva University.

Why are dividends so important? There have been many studies which have shown that a good deal of the return on stocks over the decades have come from reinvested dividends. These dividends buy additional shares which themselves grow in value and pay new dividends. This power of steady compounding is quite phenomenal, especially if you have time on your side. My father always said, "You can either have men at work, or money at work."

Good companies raise their dividends regularly. So the original 2 percent, dividend can become 2.5 percent, and then 5 percent and maybe even 150 percent of your original investment. As a physician I do not personally own Philip Morris stock, but my father-in-law worked for the company for years and he still holds considerable Philip Morris stock both inside and outside of his pension. Philip Morris is a cash-generating company that has raised its dividend phenomenally over the years. In 1977 it paid a 7-cent dividend with a yield of 2 percent a share. By now the dividend has gone up about 70-fold to $4.80. That represents an eye-popping 140 percent a year return on the

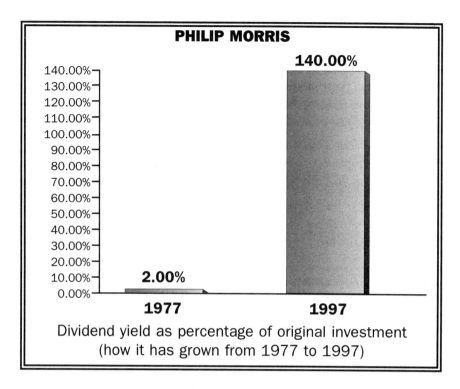

PHILIP MORRIS

140.00%

140.00%
130.00%
120.00%
110.00%
100.00%
90.00%
80.00%
70.00%
60.00%
50.00%
40.00%
30.00%
20.00%
10.00%
0.00%

2.00%

1977   **1997**

Dividend yield as percentage of original investment
(how it has grown from 1977 to 1997)

original investment. Each $1000 that Dad invested in Philip Morris in 1976 now pays $1400 a year in dividends alone. This is more than the original investment!

The stock price has gone up accordingly. The present $4.80 dividend is only yielding 4.2 percent on the current share price of $113. In 1977 a share was $3.50. (Dad tells me that he even purchased earlier shares for under a dollar.) So the stock itself has gone up 32 times over in addition to the 140 percent dividend on the original investment (see bar graph above). As I said, I do not personally own Phillip Morris stock, but on fundamentals alone it is a phenomenal stock. It helped put my wife and her siblings through college and funds Dad's retirement to this day.

Why did Philip Morris appreciate so much in price? It is common that the price of a stock goes up to reflect the new dividend. Why? Obviously a stock paying 140 percent a year would be snapped up instantly. If the price of the stock didn't go up accordingly, which lowers the yield, the yield would become so astronomically high that people would be tripping over each other to buy the stock. Over the years as a dividend is raised, and the yield is raised, people snap up the stock to get the new higher yield. This raises the price of the stock via supply and demand. This then lowers the yield to a more normal level, until the next dividend increase, when the whole cycle starts again. While the dividend yield based on the original investment may be 140 percent, which is outstanding, the same dividend based on current stock prices may be only 4.2 percent which is more normal. To your benefit, that more normal present dividend yield came about because your original investment has appreciated greatly in value.

An important point: Don't just buy a stock because it has a high current dividend yield. Perhaps the yield is high because the price of the stock has fallen due to fundamental problems in the underlying company. If the yield is high because the price is sinking, that dividend and that company may not last. If the dividend is high because the company is paying out all its profits in dividends, that is also no good. You want a company to pay out some cash in dividends but use the rest of the cash to reinvest in the business and make it grow. In the next chapter I will teach you how to analyze dividend yields and payout ratios to determine which dividends are safe and which are not.

The converse is also true. A low present dividend may be attractive if the company has a proven track record of constantly raising its dividend. In the next chapter I will teach you how to look for companies that continually raise their dividend. In Chapter 12 I will provide you with charts showing how much my companies paid out in dividends 20 years ago and how much that has grown to today. For example, the Hewlett Packard dividend in 1976 only yielded 0.3 percent. But the company has been raising the dividend at an annual rate of about 19 percent. By now the dividend on the original investment is 14 percent. I also own Intel Corp. It only started paying a small dividend in 1992 but the dividend has already quadrupled and it was announced today in the *Wall Street Journal* that it may double yet again. At that rate of increase, the original minuscule dividend may soon become very significant.

In bad times, dividends protect a stock. How is that? As the price of a stock falls, the dividend yield goes up. What was a 2 percent dividend on a $100 stock becomes a 4 percent dividend if the stock crashes to 50 or a 8 percent dividend if the stock plummets to 25. So people start buying in. They say to themselves, "Well, the stock is going down but it now pays 4 percent, so it may be worth buying at that price. I'll make 4 percent on my money while I wait for the stock to go back up." You don't want to buy into a falling company making an obsolete product such as buggy whips at 4 percent, but GE at 4 percent may be worth the gamble. Microsoft pays no dividend, so as it plummets in a falling stock market there is no compelling reason to jump on in and buy, unless you think the price itself is getting to be a real bargain. More people will jump in to buy a dividend-paying stock as the market falls than a nondividend paying stock. This tends to support the price of the dividend payers and prevent these stocks from falling too far.

This has its limits. Many New York and New England bank stocks, such as Citicorp and Bank of Boston, fell so far a few years back that their dividend yield was near or over 10 percent. But alas, even though one New England bank hadn't skipped a dividend in 200 years it did the unthinkable and did just that. So there went the 10 percent yield. And many of the New York banks had to eliminate or slash their dividend as well. IBM had a few rough years recently and as the stock price fell the dividend yield accordingly rose. But IBM also did the unthinkable and cut its once sacrosanct dividend to conserve cash. But, all in all, dividend-paying stocks will hold up better in down markets.

Dividends are also a historical judge of a stock. When you pull up stock histories on the internet on the common standard services, you usually get one year of information. The most I found were five-year histories in Barron's Online Edition. The standard print edition of Standard & Poor's gives about 10 years of history and Value Line Investment Survey gives around 15 years of past history on a stock. Data going further back are hard to find.

Standard & Poor's lists one important fact for each stock which I have not found elsewhere, namely, how many years has this stock paid an uninterrupted dividend. I may not be able to dig up stock price and earnings on GE or Bristol Myer or PNC Bank Corp beyond 15 years back, but I know that they have paid continual dividends since 1899, 1900, and 1865 respectively. That tells me a lot. These companies have been generating enough cash and earnings to pay a dividend for 100 years or more. They never stopped, even in 1929 or during the depression! Does it predict the future? Of course not. But if you hold stocks that have stayed the course for a 100 years or more and have weathered the great depression with dividend intact, then you have some degree of confidence that the future will probably be okay for these companies.

With few exceptions my stocks have paid nonstop dividends for 50-100 years or more. I also look for companies that steadily increase the dividend, as described above for Philip Morris, Intel, and Hewlett Packard. Value Line and Standard & Poor's supply dividend-increase information for 10-15 years. Many brokerage houses will supply a list of companies that consistently raise their dividends. Just today, as I type this, I checked my portfolio on Yahoo on the internet and saw a news article on the web that American Water Works, one of my stocks, has raised its dividend another 8.5 percent. Since I have owned it, the dividend has gone up on average 12.2 percent a year. It has paid nonstop since 1948 when it became a public company. On my original investment I now earn 5.88 percent a year even though the original dividend only gave me 3.96 percent a year, plus the stock has gone up 19.2 percent a year with dividends and 14.8 percent a year on capital gains alone since I first bought it five years ago. This is why it is so important to reinvest your dividends.

My oldest son Elchonan bought 10 shares each of Coke, Johnson and Johnson, and Hershey with money he received as *bar-mitzvah* presents. He promptly enrolled in their dividend reinvestment programs (DRIPS) on the advice of his wise father. These programs automatically reinvest his dividends for free and let him add small amounts, as little as $10 a month, to buy new fractional shares without commissions. He has almost doubled his shares this way in the last three years and he has more than doubled his money. If he does this until he is 65, and never invests in anything else, he could easily be a multimillionaire. One share of Coke bought at the initial public offering in 1919, with reinvested dividends, is worth over $5 million today. There are books in the library and information on the web and from your broker on which companies have dividend reinvestment or DRIP plans available for shareholders of record. These last words are very important, SHAREHOLDERS OF RECORD.

But alas, virtually all of my stocks are in my pension. Pension stocks are never held on record. Instead they are held in street name. So you could not enroll in DRIP programs in your pension; at least not five years ago. But in October 1994, my broker told me that his company had initiated a DRIP program for its pension accounts. The company itself uses the customers' stock dividends to buy shares of the underlying stocks in the open market. It then deposits, for free, into its various customers' accounts fractional shares equal to what would have been a reinvested dividend. Now I have thousands of dividend dollars going right back into my stocks for free. This single service, more than any other, almost guarantees me a large nest egg some day.

Furthermore, a DRIP program outside of a pension is taxable, but in a pension plan it is tax free. My kid must pay 15 percent tax on all his reinvested dividends, but 100 percent of my pension dividends now go to work tax free, hopefully for decades to come. Other brokerages now offer the same DRIP service on their pension accounts.

Before October 1994 I sort of invented my own DRIP in my pension. I would wait until enough cash had built up and then reinvest it, but there were disadvantages to this approach. First of all I had to wait until about $1000 in dividends had built up or the commissions would have been enormous on a small purchase. Secondly, there was always a commission to pay even when enough cash did build up. Thirdly, the process was not automatic so I really had to stay on top of my dividends and consciously reinvest them. Also, I could not buy fractional shares. With the new program it is free, it is automatic and immediate, and even fractional shares are bought. Literally every penny goes to work.

I strongly recommend the following fine books which describe in greater detail the importance of dividends, dividend information for many companies, and dividend reinvestment plans (DRIPS).[1]

1. *The Dividend Rich Investor* by Joseph Tigue and Joseph Lisanti

    This excellent book describes the importance of dividends in just about the clearest terms I have ever read. It also contains numerous charts and tables which will tell you everything you need to know about the dividend histories and growth rates of many common companies. One unique table tells you how many years you would have to hold a company's stock until the dividend grows enough to pay for the original stock. I have never seen that information elsewhere

2. *Dividends Don't Lie* by Geraldine Weiss and Jane Lowe

    Describes a unique system whereby Ms. Weiss tells you when to get in and out of stocks based on their dividend yield. Even if you are not a market timer (and I am not, I basically buy and intend to hold forever), this well-written book still explains in great detail the importance of dividends and provides much historical data.

3. *Buying Stocks Without a Broker* by Charles B. Carlson

    Everything you need to know about dividend reinvestment plans (DRIPS). Lists companies, the details of their plans, addresses, phone numbers, etc. An indispensable reference work for DRIP investors.

The following tables demonstrate how important dividends are to the total return of a portfolio. I set up my Quicken program to figure out my returns with and without dividends.

Table 1 (p. 93) shows the average annual rate of return on each of my stocks held from March 7, 1990 until December 31, 1997. Column A shows the average annual return without dividends, just on capital gains. Column B shows the average annual return including reinvested dividends and clearly demonstrates the often tremendous boost given by dividends.

---

1. see Appendix I for a more complete reading list on stocks in general.

TABLE 1		
	A. Average annual return without dividends 3/7/90—12/31/97	**B.** Average annual return including dividends 3/7/90—12/31/97
ABBOTT	17.8%	20.1%
AM. WATER	18.7%	22.9%
BOEING	16.0%	18.0%
BRISTOL-MYERS	21.0%	25.3%
CINC. BELL	26.6%	30.5%
COKE	28.8%	30.2%
CONS. GAS	9.6%	14.0%
DOVER	25.9%	27.7%
GE	29.7%	32.6%
HEINZ	16.2%	19.4%
LILLY	24.5%	28.2%
MERCK	23.7%	26.1%
3M	11.8%	14.9%
PNC	20.0%	24.3%
TECO	7.6%	12.5%
WACHOVIA	24.3%	27.7%
WISC. ENERGY	2.8%	8.0%
TOTAL PORTFOLIO	18.6%	21.9%

Note: Duke, Gillette, and Hewlett Packard have not yet been owned for a significant period of time, so they have not shown meaningful dividend returns. Microsoft does not pay dividends; Intel pays only an insignificant divident.

Table 2 (p.94) shows the total return for each individual stock with and without dividends. Column A is the total return from March 7, 1990 until Dec. 31, 1997 on capital gains alone, without dividends. Column B shows the total return for the same period with the inclusion of reinvested dividends.

EXPLANATION OF GRAPHS

The graphs on the following pages demonstrate the same information in bar form. In the first four graphs (pp. 95, 96) the

TABLE 2		
	A. **Total return** **without dividends** **3/7/90—12/31/97**	**B.** **Total return** **including dividends** **3/7/90—12/31/97**
ABBOTT	110.8%	132.7%
AM. WATER	103.4%	137%
BOEING	127.4%	150%
BRISTOL-MYERS	168.5%	226.9%
CINC. BELL	189.8%	241.4%
COKE	198.5%	214%
CONS. GAS	53%	87.4%
DOVER	162.8%	180.7%
GE	219.8%	254.9%
HEINZ	107.4%	139.9%
LILLY	262.5%	334.7%
MERCK	201.5%	236.8%
3M	58.9%	78.7%
PNC	149.9%	203.4%
TECO	38.6%	71.6%
WACHOVIA	142.5%	173.1%
WISC. ENERGY	13.2%	42.6%
TOTAL PORTFOLIO	98.6%	125%

gray bars show the average annualized return for each stock without reinvested dividends (i.e. on capital gains alone). The black bar right next to it shows the same value with reinvested dividends factored in. The second set of four graphs (pp. 97, 98) show how reinvested dividends have added to the total return on each of my stocks.

Finally there are three graphs (pp. 99, 100) which show the effects of reinvested dividends on my portfolio as a whole.

How the annualized return on my stocks was increased due to the influence of reinvested dividends:

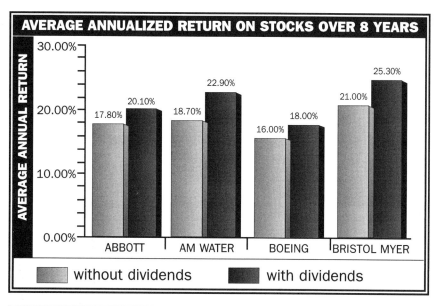

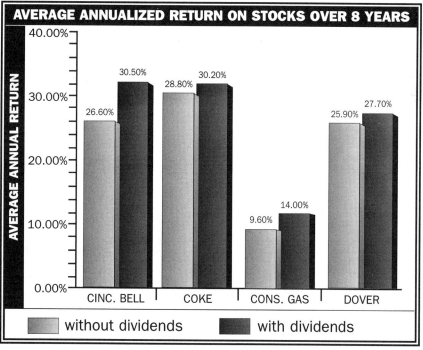

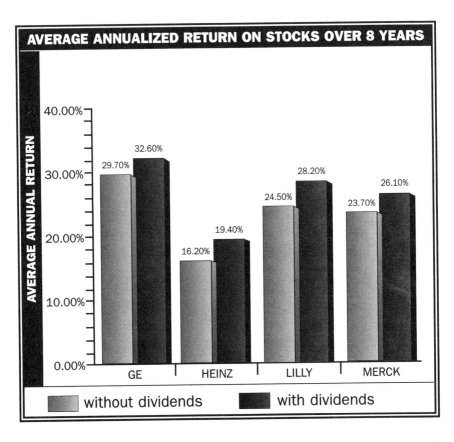

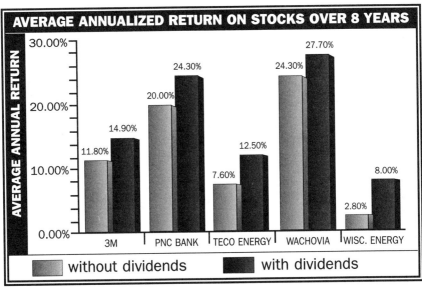

How the total return on my stocks was increased due to the
influence of reinvested dividends:

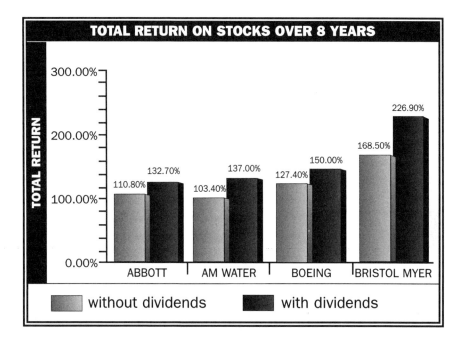

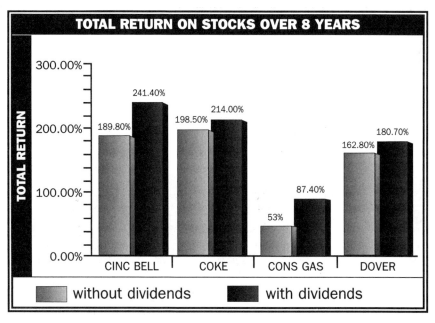

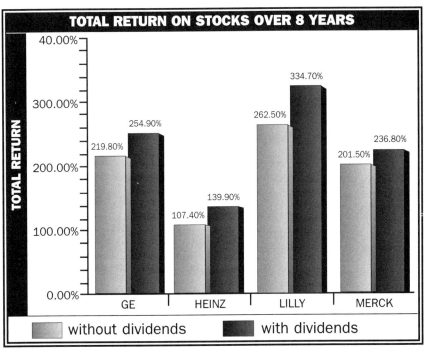

TOTAL RETURN ON STOCKS OVER 8 YEARS

Stock	without dividends	with dividends
GE	219.80%	254.90%
HEINZ	107.40%	139.90%
LILLY	262.50%	334.70%
MERCK	201.50%	236.80%

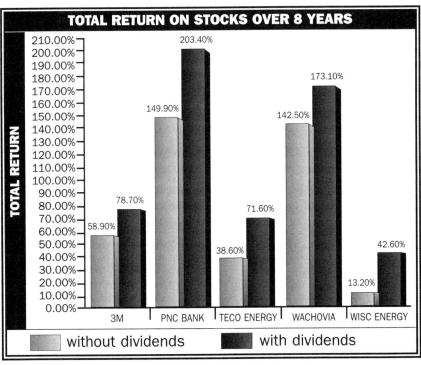

TOTAL RETURN ON STOCKS OVER 8 YEARS

Stock	without dividends	with dividends
3M	58.90%	78.70%
PNC BANK	149.90%	203.40%
TECO ENERGY	38.60%	71.60%
WACHOVIA	142.50%	173.10%
WISC ENERGY	13.20%	42.60%

How the annualized return on my stocks was increased due to the influence of reinvested dividends:

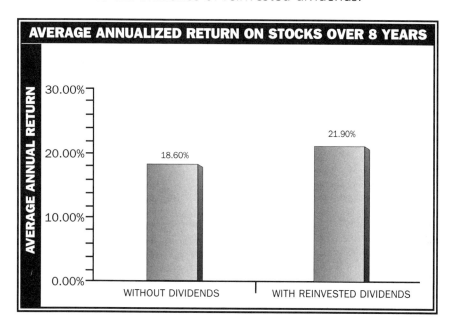

How the total return on my stocks was increased due to the influence of reinvested dividends:

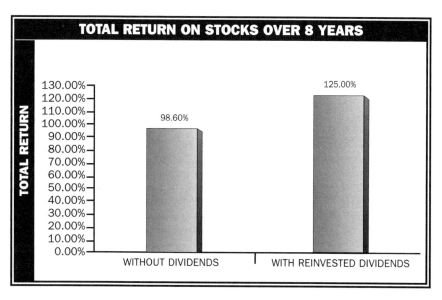

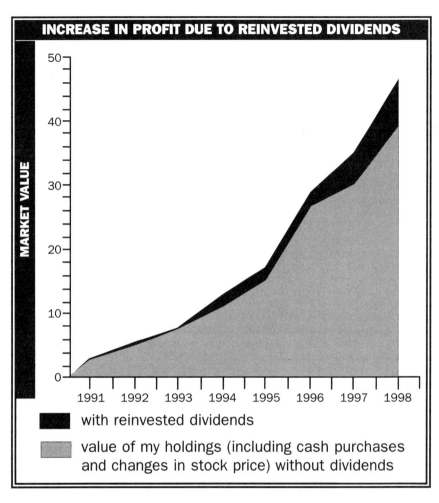

Total Portfolio

9

SIMPLE TOOLS OF FUNDAMENTAL STOCK ANALYSIS

(HOW I PICKED MY 22 STOCKS)

All my research on investing convinced me that I could do better on my own than with mutual funds. I knew that I needed solid companies, with good growth prospects, that paid a continual and rising dividend. I spent a year going through the Value Line Investment Survey in the public library. I used Standard & Poor's reports as well as other materials for back-up research. As arduous as this sounds, it did not take much more than a few hours a week.

I knew that 20 or so stocks was all that was needed to give adequate diversification (more on this below). Value Line covers approximately 1700 stocks in about 50 different industrial groupings. I checked out industries that interested me such as medical companies. As I researched a wide range of stocks, I discovered new areas of interest. Using criteria which I will explain further on in this chapter, I narrowed the potential candidates down to about 50. To make the final selection of 22 stocks I did more detailed research in Standard & Poor's, in company annual reports, or from materials supplied by my brokers. Peter Lynch said in *One Up on Wall Street* that even small investors can call companies and clarify points about the company's prospects by speaking to investment officers. I did just that and spoke to various investment officers or vice-presidents at many of the companies I own. That was actually a lot of fun.

Value Line is an indispensable guide. It helps you to screen out what you don't want and include what you do. It lists a multitude of facts about each stock, with much of the data going back for 15 years — earnings, revenues, cash flow, dividend amount, dividend yield, dividend increase rate, dividend payout ratio, returns on equity, etc. Much of this information can be found in Standard & Poor's as well. There is one item which Standard & Poor's lists, which is not in Value Line, namely, for how many years has the company continually paid dividends. This is a crucial piece of information for my stocks.

Value Line employs a unique and effective double-rating system. One rating is for the near-term outlook for the stock, rated from a best of 1 to a worst of 5. The other rating is for the safety of the company, similarly rated from 1-5. I pretty much ignored the near-term outlook ratings as I was interested in long-term investments, over decades, not months. However, for the very same reason I paid close attention to the safety rating. These were long-term investments and there may be times in the future when I would want my investments to be on auto pilot, for example if I would be studying in Israel. Standard & Poor's also gives letter grades on a company's fundamental financial strength or safety.

Value Line breaks down its universe of 1700 stocks, covering the most commonly held ones in America, into about 50 industry groupings. Before each grouping it gives a description of the industry as a whole, factors that affect it, points of analysis unique to it, etc. These are wonderful educational lessons. Every 13 weeks the information is updated. So after a full year you have read four reports on each industry and each stock. You will have learned what is important in each industry and how to analyze each industry.

In any industry you want a company that has paid a dividend for many years, preferably even during the depression, without interruption. You want the dividend payout ratio to be low, that is, the company doesn't pay out too high a percentage of earnings as dividends. You don't want a company paying out 80 percent of its earnings in dividends because that only leaves 20 percent behind for investment in future growth. It also doesn't leave much margin for error if earnings drop. You want to see a history of steadily rising dividends. You want a history of rising earnings and stock price to go along with rising dividends. You want a low level of debt and good returns on equity and capital.

A low level of debt is of crucial importance in a long-term portfolio. Why? A company can never go bankrupt with low or no debt. In the worst of recessions or even depressions, if a company does not owe the bank money it can ride out the bad times. Lay off employees, shut factories, idle the equipment, turn off the lights, and wait for economic conditions to improve. But if you owe the banks an overwhelming amount of money, you must pay principle and interest even if business is doing poorly. Making these payments when there are no earnings could bankrupt the company and your stock.

For example, Boeing traditionally has low debt. They had the misfortune to introduce the gas-guzzling 747 to the world just before the 1973 Arab oil embargo. Sales of jetliners plummeted. But with no debt, Boeing patiently waited out the bad times until jetliner orders resumed. I believe that they even had to lay off close to 100,000 workers. The company did survive, hired the workers back, and is thriving today. In fact Boeing keeps a cash horde of billions on hand to finance development of new planes. When I bought Boeing at a price of $17.5 a share, I was picking up $5 of Boeing's cash reserves for each share purchased. So each share really only cost me $12.

All in all, I enjoyed the stock research which I did. As a physician I certainly appreciate education and learning new things. Having never studied finance or investing as a kid or young adult, I found it enjoyable to educate myself in a totally new area. If you do not want to take the time to research stocks yourself, you are probably safe buying my 22 stocks, however, with the following warning. I strongly believe that all 22 together work synergistically and balance each other. Each of the 22 companies by themselves are fine stocks as well. But if you only bought one or two, I have no idea how they would perform. You could be unlucky enough to pick the one or two which may not do well over the coming decades. As a group, I believe that my portfolio of utilities, banks, consumer products, industrial and technology companies will balance out for a profitable ride. Taken individually, however, their return is harder to predict.

The other caveat is that I have not the slightest clue as to how the short-term irrational stock market will perform. You could buy one of my stocks, or all 22, and they could crash tomorrow if the market were to crash. You could lose 50 percent of your money tomorrow if you buy my stocks. If you are buying in small pieces or reinvesting your dividends, then that is actually in your favor. But no matter what, I am absolutely convinced that over 10-20-30 years these 22 stocks will return excellent returns.

Do your own research or piggyback on my year of research. Either way be prepared that tomorrow your stocks could go down 50 percent. Do not invest money in stocks unless you are in for the long term. Warren Buffett has said that anyone who can't stand to see his stocks lose 50 percent in value should not be in the stock market to begin with.

So, for the appropriately warned and ready, here are the criteria I used to pick my winning portfolio of 22 stocks.

1. Low debt

2. History of rising earnings and stock price

3. History of continual dividend payments for 50-100 years

4. History of continually raising the dividend

5. Low payout ratio of the dividend

6. Historically good returns on equity and capital

7. Dominance of an industry with well laid-out plans for future growth

8. History of product innovation with high R&D spending

9. Good diversification of product lines

10. Good foreign sales

11. Diversify the stocks among many industries and sectors

SPECIAL CRITERIA FOR ELECTRIC UTILITIES

1. Located in an economically thriving geographic area with good population growth

2. Regulatory environment where the state authorities are pro utility and pro business

3. Dividend payout ratio can be higher than for other companies

4. Debt ratio can be higher than for other companies

5. Diversified fuel mix

6. If coal burning, uses low-sulfur coal

7. If using nukes, make sure it is high-quality nukes

8. Customer base is mostly residential and commercial, not industrial

9. Company is a low-cost producer, ready to compete in the coming deregulated environment

SPECIAL CRITERIA FOR BANKS

1. Located in economically thriving geographic area

2. Conservative lending

3. Low-loan losses and good coverage of the losses

4. High-capital ratios, meeting or exceeding federal standards

If you are interested in other areas, Value Line can guide you as to which criteria to evaluate in that particular industry. Now for the details.

1. LOW DEBT

It's simple. You simply cannot go bankrupt if you don't owe money. You can wait out the bad times until good times come. Drug companies and high-tech companies, as well as Boeing, are traditionally low-debt industries. They need huge sums of cash on hand for research and development and do not want to be hampered by debt payments. As I noted above, Boeing introduced the gas-guzzling 747 just before the Arab oil embargo of the early 1970s. Orders plummeted as airlines could no longer afford the fuel to run planes nor generate profits to buy planes. With no debt, Boeing patiently waited. Eventually the crisis passed and orders picked up. If there were anxious bankers knocking on their door for debt repayments, then all the layoffs in the world and all the waiting would not have saved them from bankruptcy.

Sometimes I had to pick between two fine companies like Coca Cola and Pepsi Cola. I chose Coca Cola because of its low debt level compared to Pepsi. In general you want less than 50 percent and Pepsi's was 62 percent. Coke's was 20 percent. Most of my stocks' debt levels are even lower than that.

2. HISTORY OF RISING EARNINGS AND STOCK PRICE

This is self-evident. It is a good indication of how solid the company has been and how solid it may be expected to be. Many people pay close attention to the ratio of stock price to earnings or P/E ratio. I never have. A high P/E indicates that the stock is currently pricey, maybe too much so, and it may drop. I buy my stocks in relatively small installments over time. If I am accumulating $10,000 in a stock then I will usually buy $2,000 a year for five years or something similar. I rarely put more than $5,000 into any stock at any one time. So, I figure, sometimes I will buy at a high price, sometimes at a low price, but it will all even out over time. In addition my steadily reinvested dividends go in at high and low prices and it all evens out.

If you are going to sink a huge amount into a stock all at once then you may very well want to pay closer attention to the P/E ratios then I ever have.

3. HISTORY OF CONTINUAL DIVIDEND PAYMENTS FOR 50-100 YEARS

If a company has paid dividends for endless decades it is a good sign of past health and indicates some hope about future health. It is especially encouraging if a stock paid nonstop dividends right through the 1929 crash and the subsequent depression of the 1930s. With few exceptions my stocks have paid dividends for a minimum of 50 years, several for 100 years or more, and one all the way back to 1865.

Of course nothing is ever guaranteed. Some New England banks eliminated a dividend payment after 200 years of nonstop paying during the real estate-lending crisis of the early 1990s. Con Edison eliminated a dividend payment in the early 1970s dues to the oil crisis. It had previously paid a continual dividend since 1885.

4. HISTORY OF CONTINUALLY RAISING THE DIVIDEND

If the dividend keeps going up, chances are so are earnings and stock price. Eventually a dividend could be raised enough that you will earn more than 100 percent a year on your original investment. My father-in-law earns $1400 a year in dividends for every $1000 he put into Philip Morris stock 20 years ago. His original 7 penny, 2 percent dividend is now a dividend of $4.80, yielding a whopping 140 percent on his original investment. In the meantime his shares have appreciated 30-fold.

My dividends have been growing on average 6.5 percent a year in the eight years I have owned my 22 stocks. My original yield was 3.02 percent and it is already up to 4.7 percent. If my dividends keep growing at 6.5 percent a year, then my annual yield will soon be approaching 10 percent. A good portfolio of stocks returns about 10 percent a year on average, based on studies analyzing stocks since 1926. Therefore, I will have my 10 percent a year on dividends alone. Presumably my stock prices will appreciate in tandem to give me an even higher return.

5. LOW PAYOUT RATIO OF THE DIVIDEND

If a company earns a dollar and pays a dividend of 5 cents, then the payout ratio is 5 percent. If it earns a dollar and pays out

50 cents, then the payout ratio is 50 percent. In general you want a low payout ratio, usually in the 20-30 percent range. You don't want most of the company's earnings paid out in dividends. That leaves too little in retained earnings for research, development, marketing, construction, etc. Also there would be no margin for error if earnings were to drop one year. Then the dividend could be in danger. All of my stocks were picked with low payout ratios.

6. HISTORICALLY GOOD RETURNS ON EQUITY AND CAPITAL

Indicate past financial health and hopefully give some indication about future financial health.

7. DOMINANCE OF AN INDUSTRY WITH WELL LAID-OUT PLANS FOR FUTURE GROWTH

8. HISTORY OF PRODUCT INNOVATION WITH HIGH R&D SPENDING

9. GOOD DIVERSIFICATION OF PRODUCT LINES

10. GOOD FOREIGN SALES

You want a General Electric that is number 1 or 2 in all its areas of business, from light bulbs to locomotive engines; or a 3M that derives 30 percent of profits from products developed in house in the last five years, from Post-it-Notes to dry laser x-ray developers; or a Hewlett Packard that invents whole new markets and then dominates them, like pocket calculators or laser and ink-jet printers; or a Bristol-Myers Squibb whose consumer products are number 1 or 2 in all their product areas. There are very few drugs that sell a billion dollars worth a year. You want an Eli Lilly that sells $2 billion worth of Prozac each year.

It is also helpful to invest in companies where the barriers to entry for competitors is high. It is easy to open up a competing hamburger chain. It is difficult if not impossible to open up shop and start competing with Boeing. It takes billions of dollars to research and develop a new aircraft and highly specialized talent is required. The only reason Airbus Industries of Europe can compete with Boeing is because the governments of England, Spain, Germany, and France subsidize its multibillion-dollar losses. Chip fabrication factories cost over a billion dollars to build, so it is not very easy for someone to start competing with Intel.

High research and development (R&D) spending paves the way for future growth. Good foreign sales act as a hedge against any domestic economic downturns which could temporarily dampen the United States market. In Chapter 12 I delineate R&D spending and foreign sales for each of my stocks.

11. DIVERSIFY THE STOCKS AMONG MANY INDUSTRIES AND SECTORS

You want to diversify your stocks among different industries. Burton Malkiel in his classic book *A Random Walk Down Wall Street* proves statistically that 13-20 stocks in differing industries are all that you need to achieve virtually 100 percent of the benefits of diversification.

The theory is simple. If you have 22 drug companies, and the present administration enacts health-care reform, then all 22 will go down. Twenty-two soda companies will all be in trouble if sugar prices were to rise. But in theory and in practice, sugar prices won't affect drug prices and the federal government probably will not bring soda consumption under the wings of managed care. So you want stocks in different industries which are all affected by differing factors.

My portfolio has stocks in industries that include drugs, aerospace, elevators, food, beverage, razors, banking, chemicals, computers, and electric, gas, water and phone utilities. The factors that will make one go down should not affect another and vice versa. In a bad market (remember an IRRATIONAL market) they will all go down. In an exuberant and dangerous speculative market, perhaps like the present one, they will all go up. However, over the decades the ups and downs of each stock should occur on their individual merits and profits. And the factors that will affect the merits and profits of an aerospace company are very different than the factors which will affect a razor blade company.

SPECIAL CRITERIA FOR ELECTRIC UTILITIES

1. LOCATED IN AN ECONOMICALLY THRIVING GEOGRAPHIC AREA WITH GOOD POPULATION GROWTH

You would like a Tampa Electric in Florida where the population is booming as opposed to a utility in North Dakota. You want a Duke Power that serves the thriving Piedmont area of the Carolinas, including bustling Charlotte as opposed to a utility serving East St. Louis.

2. REGULATORY ENVIRONMENT WHERE THE STATE AUTHORITIES ARE PRO UTILITY AND PRO BUSINESS

Value Line has lists of which states favor utilities when it comes to rate increases (and therefore profit increases and stock and dividend increases) and which states favor the consumer and are against utility-rate increases. I hate to be a Scrooge toward the consumer, but as a long-term investor you want Florida and Wisconsin utilities like my Tampa Electric and Wisconsin Energy because those states are renowned for being pro-utility. You do not want utilities in New York which is anti-business, anti-utility, high tax and very pro-consumer. Sorry, Mommy and Daddy in Queens, New York. I'm glad New York protects your rights, but I won't invest in your utility.

3. DIVIDEND PAYOUT RATIO CAN BE HIGHER THAN FOR OTHER COMPANIES

4. DEBT RATIO CAN BE HIGHER THAN FOR OTHER COMPANIES

Since utilities are government regulated they are somewhat safer than regular companies. Therefore they can carry somewhat higher debt (even 50 percent or more) and pay out a greater percentage of earnings as dividends (even 70 percent). In the coming deregulated environment I do no know if this will still be true. My utilities are conservative and have low debt and low payout ratios, with room for future dividend increases. It never hurts to be a little safe.

5. DIVERSIFIED FUEL MIX

You prefer a company that generates its electricity using various fuels such as oil, gas, nuclear, hydroelectric. Why? If a company used nothing but oil, then an oil embargo can really hurt it. That is why Con Edison had to eliminate a quarterly dividend in 1973, the first time since 1885. If a company uses nothing but coal, then new federal regulations requiring cleaner emissions from coal burning could be financially devastating. Duke Power uses coal and nukes. Wisconsin Energy uses nukes, coal, gas, and hydroelectric. My only exception to this good rule is Tampa Electric. It uses almost nothing but coal. However it is clean-burning, low-sulfur coal which means that it already meets all federal regulations for the foreseeable future. If future regulations will necessitate clean-up costs, the pro-utility Florida government would most likely allow Tampa Electric to pass the costs on to its rate payers. Tampa Electric is just such a good utility that I couldn't pass on it even with its lack of fuel diversity.

6. IF COAL BURNING, USES LOW SULFUR COAL

Tampa Electric and Wisconsin Energy both use low-sulfur coal. In fact Tampa Electric mines it, transports it, and sells it to other utilities. You do not want a company burning dirty, polluting, high-sulfur coal. That company will have to spend a lot of money to put scrubbers on their power plants to reduce emissions to allowable federal levels.

7. IF USING NUKES, MAKE SURE IT IS HIGH-QUALITY NUKES

As a radiologist who spent years working with radiation, nuclear power plants do not bother me at all. My Duke Power and Wisconsin Energy have virtually the safest nuclear power plants in the country, if not the world. You do not want a Florida Power and Light or Long Island Lighting that have had past nuclear power plant problems or a Northeast Utilities which is currently struggling to survive due to financial problems brought on by a poor nuclear program.

8. CUSTOMER BASE IS MOSTLY RESIDENTIAL AND COMMERCIAL, NOT INDUSTRIAL

When the economy turns down, industry could cut back on electric usage. Residential houses and commercial stores usually use the same amount of electricity in good times and bad. So you want a Tampa Electric with 76 percent of its power going to residential and commercial users and only 16 percent to industrial users. Duke Power has an industrial usage of 33 percent, mainly to textile manufacturers in the Carolinas, which is high, but it is such a good utility that I bought it anyway.

Remember, no utility or stock will be perfect on every count. You have to weigh the positive qualities against any negative ones and choose accordingly.

9. COMPANY IS A LOW-COST PRODUCER, READY TO COMPETE IN THE COMING DEREGULATED ENVIRONMENT

The federal government will soon be overturning laws dating back to 1935 which heavily regulated the utility industry. These laws gave each electric utility a geographic area of monopoly. Competition did not exist. If a utility was inefficient at building or generating electric plants then it merely passed its inefficiencies on to its captive customers. With no competition the industry could get away with this.

Now competition is coming big time. Industries, and eventually even residential homeowners, will soon be able to pick their electric provider from anywhere in the country, just as you can now pick your long-distance telephone service. If a factory can't get cheap electricity from its local inefficient utility, then it will shop elsewhere for a more efficient, cheaper utility.

My electric utilities Wisconsin Energy, Tampa Electric, and Duke Power have all taken steps to deal with the coming deregulation. They are all low cost and efficient providers. Duke Power has a business partnership with Louis Dreyfus Energy to market wholesale gas and electricity nationwide. They just won the contract to provide electricity to Dover, Delaware for the next 10 years, beating out 22 others who submitted bids. Duke just purchased Panenergy, one of the nation's largest natural gas companies, to become an energy powerhouse selling wholesale gas and electric nationwide.

Imagine what this means to a nationwide company like Sears or WalMart. Instead of thousands of separate utility bills for each store nationwide, they could get one bill from one company that is supplying all their energy needs from coast to coast — one bill and one check to write each month to one energy provider, instead of thousands of individual ones to different local utilities — and the ability to negotiate the best price possible. You want utilities, like mine, that will be able to compete in this environment.

SPECIAL CRITERIA FOR BANKS

Banks have to meet federal criteria for safety. You want banks that meet the requirements and exceed them. You want a bank in an economically thriving area with good demand for residential mortgages and commercial loans. You want a bank smart enough to avoid faddish areas that lose billions, like loans to Latin America which almost swamped Citicorp or speculative real estate loans which did swamp the Savings and Loan industry 10 years ago. You want banks with a low level of bad loans and enough cash on hand to cover the bad loans that do crop up. Value Line can guide you to evaluate potential bank stocks for these criteria.

My two banks, PNC BankCorp and Wachovia BankCorp, meet all these criteria and are truly stellar banks with solid financial underpinnings.

10

THE
MEISTER FUND

Here is the portfolio that enabled me to retire early and sleep peacefully at night. I call it the MEISTER fund or: May Exit Intense career Soon, Taking Early Retirement. Our 22 stocks are:

UTILITIES:

Duke Energy	Tampa Electric
Wisconsin Energy	Consolidated Natural Gas
American Water Works	Cincinnati Bell Telephone

BANKS:

PNC BankCorp	Wachovia BankCorp

CONSUMER PRODUCTS:	
Coca Cola	Heinz Foods
Gillette	

PHARMACEUTICALS:	
Abbott Labs	Bristol-Myers Squibb
Eli Lilly	Merck

INDUSTRY AND TECHNOLOGY:	
Boeing	Dover Corp.
General Electric	Hewlett Packard
Minnesota Mining and Manufacturing (3M)	

NONDIVIDEND OR LOW-DIVIDEND PAYING HIGH TECH:
Intel Corp (minuscule but rapidly growing dividend)
Microsoft (no present dividend)

Note that the 22 stocks are pretty well diversified, although there is some sector weighting. There are three electric utilities, although they are diversified by geographic area. Being this is a buy and hold portfolio, the caution in me demanded slight over-weighting in conservative utilities.

There are four pharmaceutical firms. In addition, GE, 3M, and Hewlett Packard have medical-product lines. Perhaps this bias is due to my medical training. I can analyze drug companies from a professional as well as financial point of view and per-haps weighted them a little heavier as a result. In the same vein, it was my intimate knowledge with General Electric X-ray, CAT scan, ultrasound, and magnetic resonance machines which first led me to analyze that company (echoes of Peter Lynch — in-vest in what you know).

The banks are slightly weighted at two, instead of just one. This too was from personal experience. I have done my own banking and investing for years with PNC BankCorp which is what led me to invest in this fine bank. Wachovia BankCorp serviced my medical school loans and the fine service I received is what led me to research this outstanding bank further.

Finally there are the three high-tech firms (Hewlett Packard, Intel Corp. and Microsoft).

You can see that the portfolio ranges from conservative utilities (although "conservative" Cincinnati Bell is one of my top performers, more than tripling in five years) to less conservative banks and consumer products companies, to out-and-out high-tech growth companies such as Intel and Microsoft.

There was an article in the December 16, 1996 issue of *Business Week* magazine which heralded a "radical new approach" to investing that "challenges the received wisdom by which trillions of dollars have been managed for decades." Robert A. Haugen, a finance professor at the Graduate School of Management of the University of California, Irvine, did extensive research and discovered that portfolios should not be all growth or all value or all high flying or all conservative. His extensive statistical and historical research proved that a portfolio that contained some less risky, high-dividend stocks mixed in with medium risky lower-dividend stocks, and spiced up with some highfliers that pay a very low or no dividend did better over time than a portfolio that was very heavily weighted toward one group or the other.

No one stock by itself is perfect. Some stocks have good profitability. Some have good cash flow. Some have a good dividend. No one stock by itself contains every perfect characteristic. But the special combination of a finely balanced portfolio can be almost perfect. Professor Haugen compares it to soup, saying, "You have a lot of ordinary ingredients, which individually you may not even like, but put them together in the right proportions and you can make a wonderful soup." This highlights another way that the individual can beat the professionally managed mutual funds. Most funds have set criteria for selecting their stocks, perhaps selecting growth issues, or value issues, or high-tech issues. They do not finely balance between growth and value, conservative and high flying. A balanced fund may throw in some cash and bonds, but its stocks themselves are still not balanced.

However you or I as individuals can select a balanced portfolio like the ones that Professor Haugen describes. He calls them his "Super Stocks" and gives a sample portfolio containing Exxon, Loews, Mobil, Pacific Gas & Electric, Schering-Plough, Texas Instruments, RJR Nabisco Holdings, Amoco, Imperial Oil, Abbott Laboratories, TRW, Unicom, Union Carbide, UST, Genuine Parts, and Micron Technology. The diverse selection has a logic to it. Some companies such as Abbott Labs and Texas Instruments give the portfolio high profitability characteristics. The big oil companies such as Amoco, Exxon, and Mobil bring liquidity, cash flow, and dividend yield. The utilities are even more conservative and bring higher dividends.

I read the article one day while relaxing in my living room chair. I smiled to myself. Give or take, this was exactly what I had done for my family. We had 22 stocks, none of which was perfect by itself, although each was carefully selected as described in Chapter 9. Some of my stocks pay a high dividend. Some have large cash flows and profits. Some are conservative and some are high flying. Yet the combination as a whole seemed to work synergistically as we had beat the market and most mutual funds for the last eight years.

I walked across the room to the dining room table where my wife was eating lunch. I told her about the article and how we had done the same thing without even knowing that it had academic backing. She smiled too. It's nice when my wife smiles. It's even nicer when your stocks can make you and your wife both smile.

11

THE STORIES

eter Lynch has stressed in his books and articles that you should be able to clearly express, in less than a minute, to even a financially uneducated listener, why you bought stock. The story should be concise, clear, and convincing. If you are in a high-tech stock which you do not begin to fathom, you have no idea of its financial fundamentals, and you only bought it on a hot tip from a golfing buddy, there is no way you can explain in a rational way in two sentences or less why you bought it. But if you carefully researched a stock, and you understand its business, the overall industry its in, and its financial fundamentals, then a brief rational synopsis is easy. Here are the one-minute stories on each of my stocks. For further details, consult the next chapter for The Rest of the Stories.

All of the companies which I selected for my portfolio are financially solid based on the fundamentals of analysis described previously (see Chapter 9). I will therefore not reiterate that each company has sound financial fundamentals. That is to be self-understood.

ABBOTT LABS

Longstanding pharmaceutical company with excellent drugs, good pipeline of new drugs, good nutritional business, and a dominant blood-testing business.

AMERICAN WATER WORKS

Largest U.S. publicly owned water utility providing an essential element to business and individuals, covering a geographic area from New Hampshire to California.

BOEING

Largest commercial airline manufacturer in the world with $^2/_3$ of the world market. High barriers of entry for any new competition. Dominant in space and defense work as well.

BRISTOL-MYERS SQUIBB

There are very few drugs in the world that sell a billion dollars worth a year. Bristol-Myers has one drug selling $1.5 billion a year, and four which sell $500 million a year. Good new-drug pipeline. Also very dominant in consumer products, such as Clairol, Ban, Keri Lotion, etc.

CINCINNATI BELL

Local phone company with very modern infrastructure utilizing mostly digital switches. Information subsidiary dominates in creating billing software which is used by the vast majority of cellular phone and cable TV companies nationwide. Also dominates in telemarketing domestically and overseas.

COCA COLA

One share bought in 1919 and held until today with reinvested dividends is worth over $5 million. If every Chinese and Indian person could be persuaded to drink one Coke a day I'd be a very rich man. Just the incremental increase in Coke sales in Texas last year was greater than total Snapple sales from coast to coast!

CONSOLIDATED NATURAL GAS

One of the largest integrated gas companies in America with both exploration and distribution units. Expanding into whole-sale electricity sales as well to serve as a one-stop energy source in the upcoming deregulated market.

DOVER CORPORATION

Second-largest elevator manufacturer in the U.S. with diver-sification into hundreds of other industrial manufacturing areas. Well run with decentralized, entrepreneurial management.

DUKE POWER

Electric utility in a growing economic area of the Carolinas with a world-renowned reputation for power plant engineering, including nuclear power plants. Designs and builds power plants for other utilities worldwide. On the forefront of wholesale electric and gas marketing in the deregulated marketplace.

GENERAL ELECTRIC

Largest capitalized company in the world, diversified from light bulbs to jet engines, from plastics to CAT scanners. Num-ber one or two in all its businesses. Has never had an operating loss in over 100 years.

GILLETTE

Dominates a world market where billions of men have to shave each morning. Just acquired Duracell Battery to extend its marketing and distribution to this other point of purchase product.

HEINZ FOOD

Dominates in diversified food areas such as condiments, tuna, frozen potatoes, infant food, pet food and Weight Watch-ers. Only company in U.S. to have 25 uninterrupted years of profit-margin increase between 1965 and 1990.

HEWLETT PACKARD

Innovative, diversified technology company that creates new markets and then dominates them, such as inventing pocket calculators or ink-jet and laser printers. A wonderful corporate citizen for its employees and for the country.

INTEL

Dominates microprocessor chip market. Probably the finest manufacturer of any product anywhere in the world.

LILLY

Hundred-year-old drug company which pioneered insulin and continues to pioneer new drugs from antibiotics to Prozac. Taking proactive steps to deal with managed care. Prozac alone sells over $2 billion worth a year.

MERCK

Dominant pharmaceutical giant with dominant drugs from vaccines to cholesterol-lowering agents. Good pipeline of new drugs. Dominant in veterinary drugs. Taking very positive steps to deal with managed care.

MICROSOFT

Dominant software company in the world. Pays no dividend and technically does not belong in my portfolio. The real reason I bought it is that my computer-savvy wife recommended it, even though it pays no dividend. What can I say? It has more than septupled in less than five years.

MINNESOTA MINING AND MANUFACTURING

Diversified innovative company which has a corporate goal of achieving 30 percent of yearly profits from discoveries made in the last five years. Innovations have ranged from inventing sandpaper to adhesive tape to dry laser x-ray printers.

PNC BANKCORP

Dominant mid-Atlantic bank with many innovative banking products from Private Banking to discount brokerage to trust management. Just won a contract to market banking services to 34-million AAA members nationwide. I am a longstanding satisfied customer. I actually picked this stock one week before Warren Buffett did!!!

TECO ENERGY

Electric utility in a growing geographic area of northern Florida. State regulators are friendly to utilities. Well diversified into independent power plants, computerized energy management, coal mining and transport, and gas exploration.

WACHOVIA BANKCORP

Dominant bank serving a thriving area of the Carolinas as well as Atlanta, Georgia. I am a satisfied customer, as they administered my medical student loans for years.

WISCONSIN ENERGY

Electric and gas utility in a state that is friendly to utilities. Good fuel mix including nuclear power plants which are among the safest and best run in the nation. Well positioned to deal with upcoming deregulation of the industry.

12

THE REST OF THE STORIES

n this chapter you will find detailed descriptions of each of my 22 stocks explaining their strengths and why I purchased them. Each of the stocks has strong financial fundamentals in accordance with the principles I outlined in Chapter 9. Therefore I will not repeat and enumerate for each stock the strengths of low-debt levels, good returns on equity, growing earnings, etc. Take my word that each one had a history of financial strength when I bought it and hopefully will continue that way. In this chapter I intend to describe to you what is unique about each stock and why each one should be considered for long-term growth and dividends.

I make an exception for dividend information. As dividends are so important to the success of my portfolio, I give detailed history of each stock's dividend. This includes:

1. how long the dividend has been paid
2. the dividend amount and yield in 1977
3. the dividend amount today and what the yield would be today on the original investment if someone had purchased the stock 20 years ago
4. the dividend growth rate for the last 10 years, and for the years that I have held the stock (usually around eight years and counting)
5. my original yield and the yield to which my dividend has grown in relation to my original investment in about eight years

SOME NOTES ABOUT THE GRAPHS

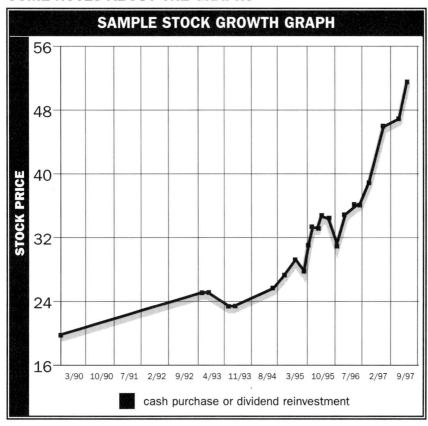

SAMPLE STOCK GROWTH GRAPH

STOCK PRICE

56
48
40
32
24
16

3/90 10/90 7/91 2/92 9/92 4/93 11/93 8/94 3/95 10/95 7/96 2/97 9/97

■ cash purchase or dividend reinvestment

This type of graph shows the growth in the stock price since I have held the investment. The important point is not that these stocks keep going up. Most stocks are going up these past few years. Sometime in the future these stocks may go down as well, even for long periods. These charts should emphasize to you the importance of REINVESTING DIVIDENDS.

The first few points on each graph show where I made original cash purchases of stock. All the many dots that follow on each graph are where dividends reinvested for free in additional shares. Notice how many dots there are in the later years on each chart. The free reinvested dividends really add up. See how they reinvested whether the stock price was up or down. Shares picked up when the stock declined or stayed level were often my most profitable ones.

SAMPLE GRAPH SHOWING VALUE OF REINVESTED DIVIDENDS

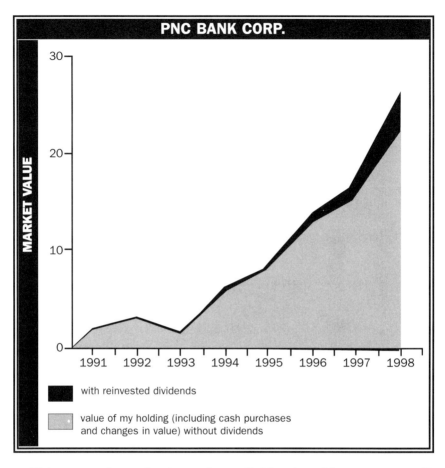

This type of graph shows how dividends add to my overall profits. The lightly shaded gray area shows the market value of the stock without reinvested dividends (i.e., on capital gains and cash purchases alone). The added black area shows the extra profit which results through reinvested dividends. Notice how the black area becomes larger and larger as time progresses. For most stocks I am only eight years out and counting. In another 20 years the black area should be huge. For some stocks the extra profit from dividends may someday be larger than the gain from capital gains. (NOTE — I have purposely omitted the zeros from the market values shown on the y-axis — feel free to add as many zeros as you'd like, the more the better.)

SAMPLE BAR GRAPH SHOWING HOW DIVIDENDS CAN GROW OVER THE YEARS TO REPRESENT A VERY LARGE RETURN ON YOUR ORIGINAL INVESTMENT

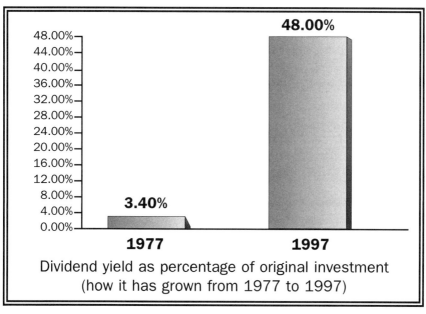

Dividend yield as percentage of original investment
(how it has grown from 1977 to 1997)

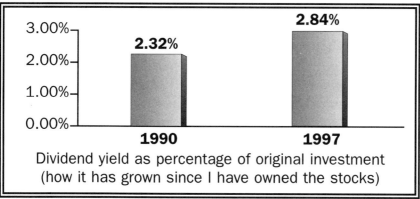

Dividend yield as percentage of original investment
(how it has grown since I have owned the stocks)

These bar graphs demonstrate the important concept of how a continually rising dividend eventually becomes very large as a percentage of the original investment (see Chapter 6). The top bar graph on the page shows how the dividend has grown in the two decades from 1977 to 1997. Take Boeing for example. The dividend was 3.4 percent in 1977 and has grown so many fold that today the dividend on an investment made in

1977 would be paying 48 percent on the original investment. In other words, if a person invested $1000 in Boeing in 1977 he would have originally received $34 per year in dividends. Today that investor would be receiving $480 for each $1000 invested.

The lower bar graph shows how the dividend has grown in the eight or so years during which I have owned the stock. Obviously the growth in eight years is less than in two decades. But you can see that my dividends are steadily going up and up. Some have already almost doubled in just eight years.

ABBOTT LABS

Abbott Labs is a diversified pharmaceutical company. Its portfolio of drugs includes the antibiotics Erythromycin and Biaxin, Lupron for treating prostate cancer, Urokinase which radiologists such as myself use to dissolve blood clots in the body, and Survanta for treating hyaline membrane disease in premature babies, also known as RDS (the disease from which President Kennedy's newborn son died in 1962). There is a good pipeline for new drugs for treatment of ulcers, AIDS, epilepsy, and prostate enlargement.

Abbott is also an industry leader in intravenous and oral nutritional supplements, including Similac and Pedialyte for infants and Ensure for adults. In addition to general supplements, Abbott also supplies unique supplements for various disease conditions which require special nutrition. Abbott also designs pumps for infusing nutritional supplements and medications into the body at predetermined rates and dosages. One of its machines can infuse four separate drugs into the body at different doses and at different times.

It also has exceptional and world-dominant strength in the area of medical diagnostics, ranging from simple one-step blood tests to the design and manufacture of complicated machinery for the simultaneous performance of numerous blood tests. Abbott's machines and diagnostics can test for toxicology, therapeutic drug levels, transplant factors, routine blood chemistry, hepatitis, AIDS, cancer, thyroid problems, fertility problems, hematology, and much more. Abbott has dominant strength in DNA testing. Recognizing DNA testing as the future in all diagnostic areas, Abbott has the highest degree of automated DNA tests in the world.

Drugs and nutritional products account for 56 percent of sales while hospital and laboratory equipment accounts for 44 percent. Foreign business accounts for 40 percent of sales and Research and Development accounts for 11 percent of sales for a whopping $1.1 dollars a year.

DIVIDEND HISTORY: ABBOTT LABS	
1. CONTINUOUS UNINTERRUPTED DIVIDEND PAID SINCE:	1926
2. DIVIDEND PAID IN 1977	$0.03
3. DIVIDEND YIELD IN 1977	2%
4. DIVIDEND PAID IN 1997	$0.96
5. 1997 DIVIDEND YIELD BASED ON ORIGINAL INVESTMENT	64%!
6. ANNUAL DIVIDEND GROWTH RATE FOR LAST TEN YEARS	17.5%
7. ANNUAL DIVIDEND GROWTH SINCE I BOUGHT THE STOCK	13%
8. MY ORIGINAL YIELD	2.14%
9. MY PRESENT YIELD ON ORIGINAL INVESTMENT	3.62%

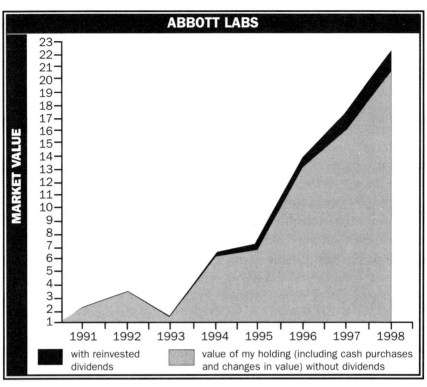

ABBOTT LABS

MARKET VALUE

- with reinvested dividends
- value of my holding (including cash purchases and changes in value) without dividends

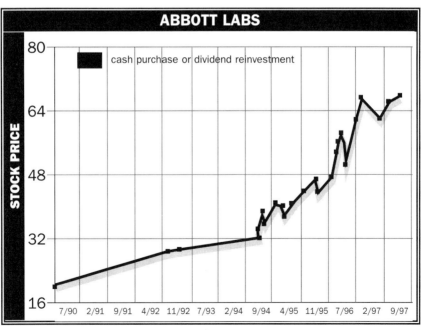

ABBOTT LABS

STOCK PRICE

cash purchase or dividend reinvestment

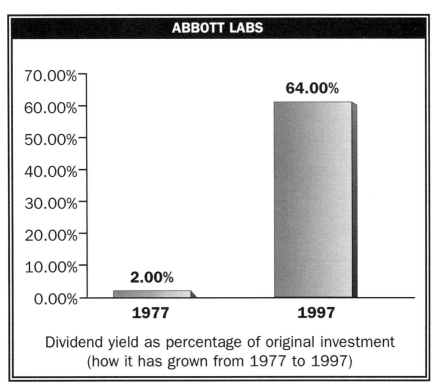

ABBOTT LABS

64.00%

2.00%

1977 **1997**

Dividend yield as percentage of original investment
(how it has grown from 1977 to 1997)

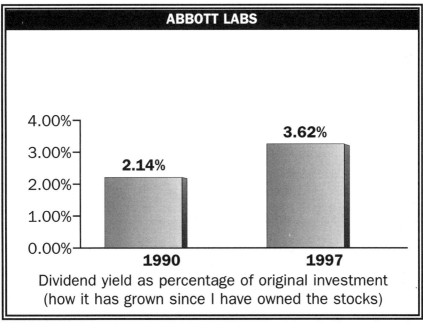

ABBOTT LABS

3.62%

2.14%

1990 **1997**

Dividend yield as percentage of original investment
(how it has grown since I have owned the stocks)

AMERICAN WATER WORKS

American Water Works is the largest investor-owned water utility in the country. It is a utility that provides the one essential ingredient that no person and no business can do without — a safe clean supply of water. It has a diversified service area stretching from New Hampshire to California. This diversified geographic coverage is a good hedge against local weather, politics, or other problems which could arise in one locale.

New federal regulations on safety and cleanliness make it harder and harder for local municipalities to keep up their own water systems. Therefore, many of them turn to American Water Works to run their water systems or to buy them out. This is a source of steady growth for the company.

American Water Works played a major role in helping Milwaukee last year after disease-causing organisms were found in its municipal water supply, causing many illnesses

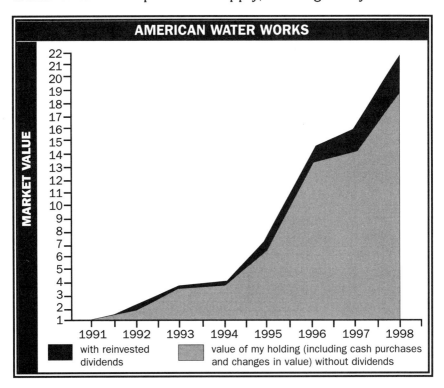

AMERICAN WATER WORKS

MARKET VALUE

1991 1992 1993 1994 1995 1996 1997 1998

with reinvested dividends

value of my holding (including cash purchases and changes in value) without dividends

DIVIDEND HISTORY:AMERICAN WATER WORKS	
1. CONTINUOUS UNINTERRUPTED DIVIDEND PAID SINCE:	1948
2. DIVIDEND PAID IN 1977	$0.09
3. DIVIDEND YIELD IN 1977	7%
4. DIVIDEND PAID IN 1997	$0.76
5. 1997 DIVIDEND YIELD BASED ON ORIGINAL INVESTMENT	59.00%!
6. ANNUAL DIVIDEND GROWTH RATE FOR LAST 10 YEARS	10.50%
7. ANNUAL DIVIDEND GROWTH SINCE I BOUGHT THE STOCK	12.20%
8. MY ORIGINAL YIELD	3.96%
9. MY PRESENT YIELD ON ORIGINAL INVESTMENT	5.88%

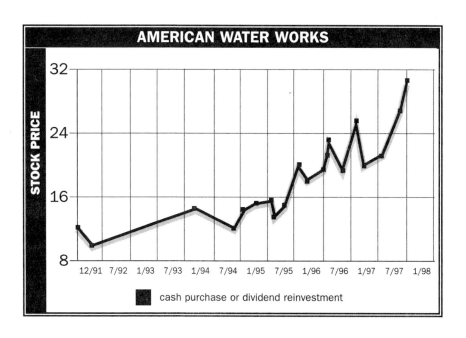

cash purchase or dividend reinvestment

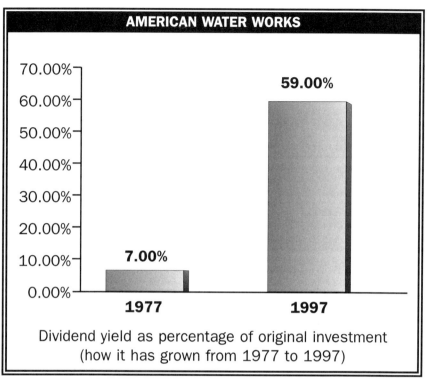

AMERICAN WATER WORKS

7.00% — 1977
59.00% — 1997

Dividend yield as percentage of original investment
(how it has grown from 1977 to 1997)

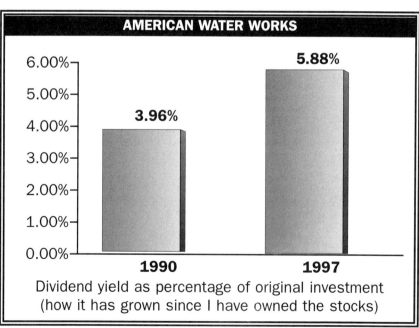

AMERICAN WATER WORKS

3.96% — 1990
5.88% — 1997

Dividend yield as percentage of original investment
(how it has grown since I have owned the stocks)

in the local population. It again played a major helping role when many Midwestern water systems were swamped with sewage as a result of the great Mississippi River flooding of 1994.

BOEING

Boeing commands 66 percent of the world commercial jetliner market. The barriers of entry for any competitor are very high. It takes countless billions of dollars and very deep talent to design and build a new jetliner. The new Boeing 777 cost billions to develop and build and revolutionized computerized design and construction. It is the first airplane ever to be totally designed by computer. Boeing's only real competitor today is Airbus Industries, the European consortium, which is backed by four European governments. The only reason Airbus poses any competition at all is that the governments of England, Spain, France, and Germany are heavily subsidizing the gigantic multibillion dollar losses that this company has incurred . If Airbus had to conform to normal market forces, it would have gone bankrupt years ago.

Boeing is big in defense work and became even more dominant this year with the purchase of the defense parts of Rockwell International and with its merger with McDonnell Douglas. Defense work includes AWACS, Comanche Helicopters, and the F-22 fighter in conjunction with Lockheed Martin. Boeing is a semifinalist in the present competition to win the $200 billion contract for the Joint Advanced Strike Technology fighter plane.

Boeing also has a presence in outer space with a position as prime contractor on the NASA space station. With its Rockwell acquisition it becomes the prime contractor on the Space Shuttle. Boeing is working on a sea platform for launching satellites.

International business accounts for 42 percent of sales. Research and development uses 6.5 percent of sales. Boeing's backlog of orders for jetliners is over $50 billion and has even approached $100 billion in the past.

DIVIDEND HISTORY: BOEING

1. CONTINUOUS UNINTERRUPTED DIVIDEND PAID SINCE:	1942
2. DIVIDEND PAID IN 1977	$0.08
3. DIVIDEND YIELD IN 1977	3.40%
4. DIVIDEND PAID IN 1997	$1.12
5. 1997 DIVIDEND YIELD BASED ON ORIGINAL INVESTMENT	48%!
6. ANNUAL DIVIDEND GROWTH RATE FOR LAST 10 YEARS	9%
7. ANNUAL DIVIDEND GROWTH SINCE I BOUGHT THE STOCK	2.60%
8. MY ORIGINAL YIELD	2.32%
9. MY PRESENT YIELD ON ORIGINAL INVESTMENT	2.84%

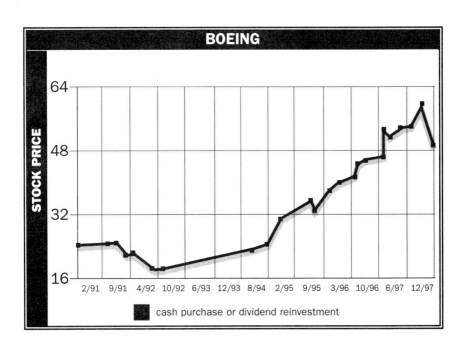

cash purchase or dividend reinvestment

146 □ THE MEISTER PLAN

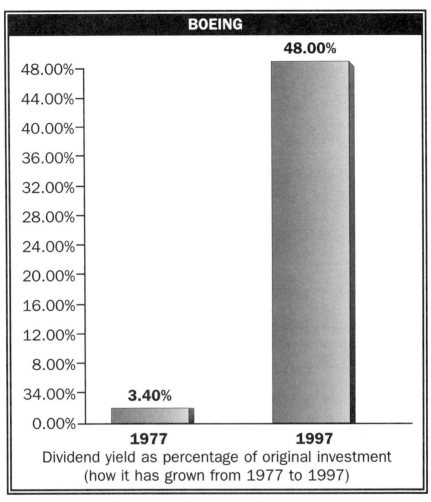

BOEING

48.00%

48.00%
44.00%
40.00%
36.00%
32.00%
28.00%
24.00%
20.00%
16.00%
12.00%
8.00%
34.00%
0.00%

3.40%

1977   **1997**

Dividend yield as percentage of original investment
(how it has grown from 1977 to 1997)

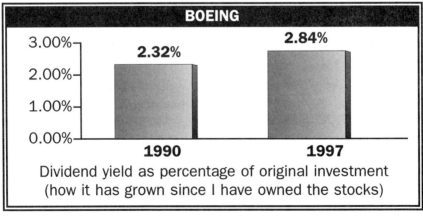

BOEING

3.00%
2.00%
1.00%
0.00%

2.32%   **2.84%**

1990   **1997**

Dividend yield as percentage of original investment
(how it has grown since I have owned the stocks)

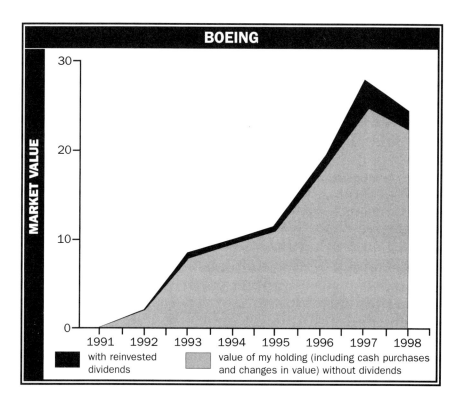

BOEING

MARKET VALUE

with reinvested dividends

value of my holding (including cash purchases and changes in value) without dividends

BRISTOL-MYERS SQUIBB

Bristol-Myers Squibb is a pharmaceutical powerhouse that is also extensively diversified into consumer products. Actually, Bristol-Myers and Squibb merged in the 1980s to form the combined company. That is why my dividend information is dated from 1982, although the separate companies have paid dividends since 1900.

There are very few billion-dollar selling drugs in the world. Bristol-Myers Squibb developed the antihypertensive drug Capoten, which sells $1.5 billion worth annually. Four other drugs sell $500 million annually and a whopping 60 products sell over $50 million per year. These dominant drugs include treatments for high cholesterol, high blood pressure, cancer, AIDS, dermatological problems, and central nervous system disorders. It sells x-ray dyes which I have personally used for years.

What sets it apart from other pharmaceutical companies is its extensive line of personal consumer products such as Clairol Hair Coloring, Excedrin and Bufferin aspirin, Keri lotion, Ban roll-on, Nuprin, a full line of infant formulas such as Enfamil, Nutramigen, and ProSobee, as well as the adult nutritional supplement Sustacal. Virtually all of its consumer products are ranked first or second in their markets. People will buy these products in good times and bad and this balances out the somewhat higher risk of the pharmaceutical end of the business.

Foreign business accounts for 44 percent of sales and Research and Development for 8.7 percent or a whopping $1.2 billion a year.

DIVIDEND HISTORY: BRISTOL-MYERS SQUIBB	
1. CONTINUOUS UNINTERRUPTED DIVIDEND PAID SINCE:	1900
2. DIVIDEND PAID IN 1982	$0.53
3. DIVIDEND YIELD IN 1982	3.60%
4. DIVIDEND PAID IN 1997	$3.04
5. 1997 DIVIDEND YIELD BASED ON ORIGINAL INVESTMENT	21%!
6. ANNUAL DIVIDEND GROWTH RATE FOR LAST 10 YEARS	14%
7. ANNUAL DIVIDEND GROWTH SINCE I BOUGHT THE STOCK	3%
8. MY ORIGINAL YIELD	4.25%
9. MY PRESENT YIELD ON ORIGINAL INVESTMENT	5.96%

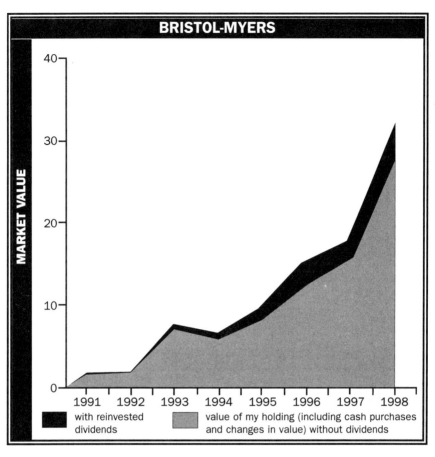

BRISTOL-MYERS

with reinvested dividends

value of my holding (including cash purchases and changes in value) without dividends

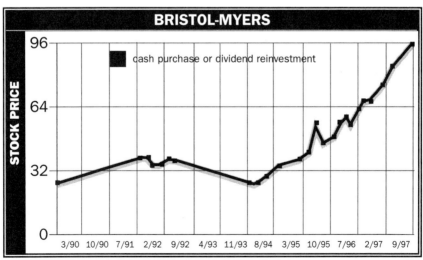

BRISTOL-MYERS

cash purchase or dividend reinvestment

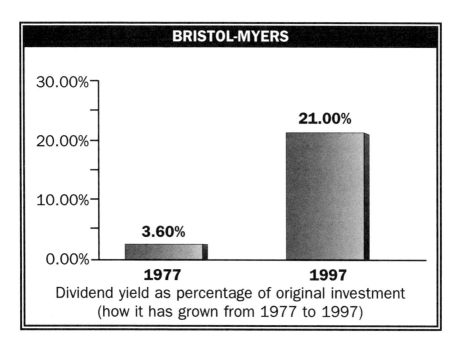

BRISTOL-MYERS

Dividend yield as percentage of original investment
(how it has grown from 1977 to 1997)

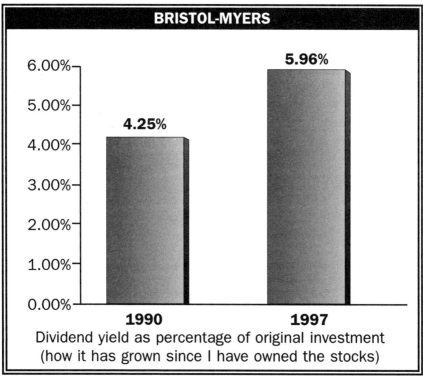

BRISTOL-MYERS

Dividend yield as percentage of original investment
(how it has grown since I have owned the stocks)

CINCINNATI BELL TELEPHONE

Cincinnati Bell Telephone is one of the oldest local telephone companies in the country, over 100 years old. Unlike the other Baby Bells, it was never part of ATT. It has a solid local phone franchise in Ohio with 960,000 access lines and a modern infrastructure with almost 90 percent of its switches already digital, far ahead of most other Baby Bells.

But its other areas of expertise fascinated me. Unlike some companies which diversify into poorly understood fields unrelated to their core business with disastrous results (what Peter Lynch calls "deworseification"), Cincinnati Bell carefully and methodically diversified into areas related to telecommunications where it could dominate.

For example? Cincinnati Bell Information Systems (CBIS) creates and provides the billing software for cellular calls made in 23 of the 25 largest calling markets in the country. CBIS also supplies the billing software for Sprint Spectrum. Cellular phone bills are extremely complex to track and calculate as the moving phone passes from cell to cell. Cincinnati Bell dominates in this area and the vast majority of cellular phone bills in this country are generated on software designed by Cincinnati Bell, over 260 million a year. The software is proprietary and hard for a newcomer to duplicate. So Cincinnati Bell gets to benefit from the torrid growth of cellular, without having to invest in the massive hardware and infrastructure of the cellular companies.

Cincinnati Bell uses the same expertise to generate many of the cable television bills generated nationwide. Again, they benefit from a related telecommunications area without the necessary huge investment in hardware needed to be a core player. They make their money quietly in the background by providing the software infrastructure needed to make the industry run.

Cincinnati Bell has a subsidiary called Mattrixx Marketing. They perform outgoing and incoming telemarketing services for the many of America's leading corporations who find it more efficient to outsource the work. They are dominant in America and overseas in Europe. They handle over 200 million calls a

DIVIDEND HISTORY: CINCINNATI BELL	
1. CONTINUOUS UNINTERRUPTED DIVIDEND PAID SINCE:	1879
2. DIVIDEND PAID IN 1977	$0.20
3. DIVIDEND YIELD IN 1977	7.50%
4. DIVIDEND PAID IN 1997	$0.80
5. 1997 DIVIDEND YIELD BASED ON ORIGINAL INVESTMENT	30%!
6. ANNUAL DIVIDEND GROWTH RATE FOR LAST 10 YEARS	7.50%
7. ANNUAL DIVIDEND GROWTH SINCE I BOUGHT THE STOCK	0%
8. MY ORIGINAL YIELD	4.04%
9. MY PRESENT YIELD ON ORIGINAL INVESTMENT	5.21%

year. When you call an 800 number to order from, question, or complain to a major American corporation, chances are you are speaking to a Cincinnati Bell employee of Mattrixx Marketing. Just recently, Mattrixx Marketing won a large overseas contract from American Express to provide for customer needs in Europe. This contract alone will require the hiring of an additional 150 people to service it.

Cincinnati Bell is so technologically advanced in all areas of telecommunications that when the massive state-owned Japanese phone system, Nippon Telephone and Telegraph, wanted to update their system, they brought Cincinnati Bell over to do it for them. Sweden and other countries have done similarly.

The present telecommunications market in America can by divided up as follows:

1. Transport, a $200 billion a year market, growing at 5-10 percent a year

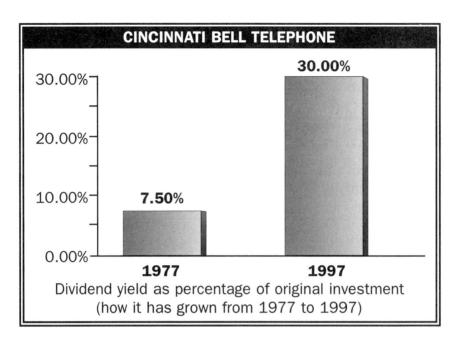

CINCINNATI BELL TELEPHONE

Dividend yield as percentage of original investment
(how it has grown from 1977 to 1997)

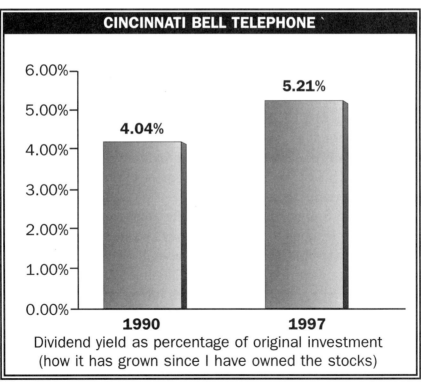

CINCINNATI BELL TELEPHONE

Dividend yield as percentage of original investment
(how it has grown since I have owned the stocks)

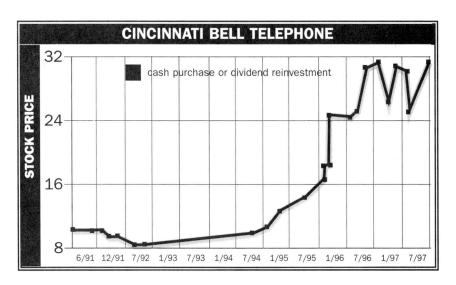

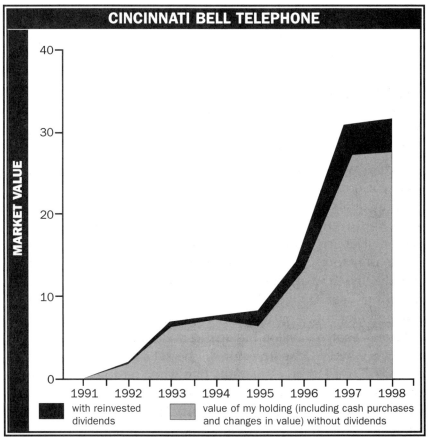

2. Content, a $100 billion a year market, growing at 10-15 percent a year
3. Support Services, a $50 billion a year market, growing at 15-20 percent a year

Cincinnati Bell core telephone business is strong in transport, Cincinnati Bell Information Services (billing software) dominates in content, and the Mattrixx Marketing subsidiary dominates in support services. The latter two areas are nonregulated and already account for 35 percent of income.

COCA-COLA

What can I say to praise the "real thing" that hasn't been already said? Most people are well aware that Coca-Cola has come a long way from its humble beginnings as a "stomach wash" formulated in Doc Pemberton's Atlanta basement to the most widely recognized trademark in the world today. Can anything be simpler? People need about 64 fluid ounces of liquid daily to survive. Worldwide Coca-Cola consumption supplies less than two of those ounces daily, so there is still plenty of room for growth.

Individuals in countries like America, Mexico, Israel, Australia and even Norway consume almost one coke a day per person. But in China, with 1.2 billion people, the populace drinks only four cokes per capita per year. In the subcontinent of India the 936 million people average only two cokes per capita per year. Unlike other companies, no high-tech invention is needed for future growth. Just convince the billion-plus Chinese and nearly a billion Indians to drink one coke a day and I and every other Coke investor will be set for life. The president of Coca-Cola, Don Ivestor, says that when he thinks of heaven he thinks of Indonesia. Why? It is the largest Muslim country in the world (where alcohol is forbidden), it is in a hot climate, and the local water supply is not the purest. The population is 198

DIVIDEND HISTORY: COCA-COLA	
1. CONTINUOUS UNINTERRUPTED DIVIDEND PAID SINCE:	1893
2. DIVIDEND PAID IN 1977	$0.06
3. DIVIDEND YIELD IN 1977	3.10%
4. DIVIDEND PAID IN 1997	$0.50
5. 1997 DIVIDEND YIELD BASED ON ORIGINAL INVESTMENT	28%!
6. ANNUAL DIVIDEND GROWTH RATE FOR LAST 10 YEARS	13%
7. ANNUAL DIVIDEND GROWTH SINCE I BOUGHT THIS STOCK	13.10%
8. MY ORIGINAL YIELD	1.56%
9. MY PRESENT YIELD ON ORIGINAL INVESTMENT	2.34%

million and the per capita consumption of coke is only eight per year. A true heaven for Coca-Cola marketers.

Coca-Cola loves to print amazing statistics in its annual report, such as how many times the number of cokes sold each year could stretch to the moon and back, etc. The one I found most amazing in last year's annual report was that the incremental unit volume growth in Texas last year was greater than all the Snapple consumed nationwide. Just the INCREASE in Coke consumed in Texas last year compared to two years ago was more than the total Snapple imbibed from sea to sea!

On a personal note, I attended the Coca-Cola annual shareholders meeting last year with my oldest son Elchonan. He owns ten shares of Coca-Cola, bought with money he received as *bar-mitzvah* presents, and he reinvests his dividends. He has more than doubled his money in less than three years. He was home from yeshiva for Pesach break and the annual meeting was in Wilmington, Delaware which is just 90 minutes north of

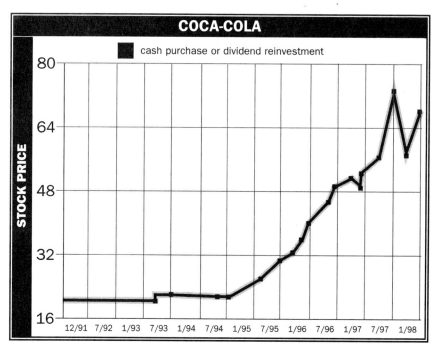

COCA-COLA

■ cash purchase or dividend reinvestment

STOCK PRICE

80 — 64 — 48 — 32 — 16

12/91 7/92 1/93 7/93 1/94 7/94 1/95 7/95 1/96 7/96 1/97 7/97 1/98

our home in Baltimore. I thought we would both enjoy attending. I also wanted to meet Warren Buffett, Coke's largest shareholder, in person and my son wanted to meet Peter Ueberroth. Mr. Ueberroth is a former baseball commissioner and he was in charge of running the 1984 summer Olympics in Los Angeles. He is now on the Coca-Cola board of directors. I got Warren Buffet to autograph my annual report (he almost took my pen by accident — I guess that's one way to become a billionaire) and my son received an autographed baseball from Mr. Ueberroth.

It also turns out that I was able to be the secret savior of American Jewry's thirst at the meeting. When it came time for the question-and-answer period I noticed that not all the shareholder questions were earth shattering or particularly deep or complex. Therefore I was emboldened to step to the microphone (much to my son's embarrassment) and ask my own question. Little shareholder me faced Roberto Goizueta (the Chairman and CEO of Coke), Warren Buffett, and Don Ivestor (the company's President and CEO) and asked the following:

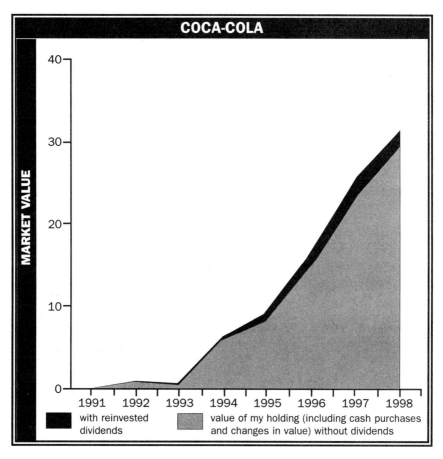

COCA-COLA

MARKET VALUE

40 —
30 —
20 —
10 —
0 —

1991 1992 1993 1994 1995 1996 1997 1998

■ with reinvested dividends

▨ value of my holding (including cash purchases and changes in value) without dividends

"Sirs, my son and I came up for the day to attend the meeting as we are both shareholders and he has Passover vacation from school. As you well know, Orthodox Jews only eat and drink kosher products and Coke is indeed kosher. However, for Passover we drink specially formulated Coke that contains no corn syrup or leavening ingredients. We tried to buy some Coke in Baltimore for the trip up. All the shopkeepers told us that this year there was not enough Kosher for Passover Coke to go around and basically the supply was consumed by the large Jewish market in New York City and there was none available for the rest of the country! In years past there was always an abundance of Kosher for Passover Coke nationwide. This is the first year in anyone's memory that Coca-Cola had not made enough Kosher for Passover

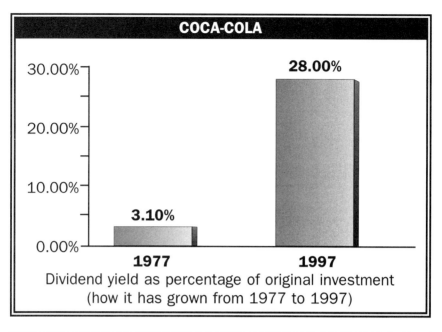

COCA-COLA

30.00%

28.00%

20.00%

10.00%

3.10%

0.00%

1977   1997

Dividend yield as percentage of original investment
(how it has grown from 1977 to 1997)

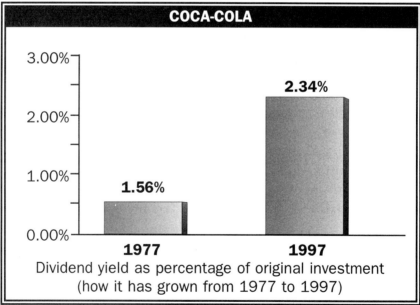

COCA-COLA

3.00%

2.34%

2.00%

1.00%

1.56%

0.00%

1977   1997

Dividend yield as percentage of original investment
(how it has grown from 1977 to 1997)

Coke. Would it be possible to correct the situation for next Passover?"

I was given a detailed answer from the aforementioned big shots who assured me that they were on top of the situation and well aware of the nationwide shortage of Kosher for Passover Coke. The president himself took out a little note pad and made several memos to address it further as soon as he returned to Atlanta. Needless to say, the following year there was a nationwide abundance of Kosher L'Pesach Coca-Cola.

In addition to sodas, Coca-Cola is also the world's largest distributor of juice products with Minute Maid and Hi-C. Foreign sales account for 70 percent of sales and 82 percent of profits.

CONSOLIDATED NATURAL GAS

Consolidated Natural Gas (CNG) is one of the largest fully integrated natural gas companies in America. It originally started as a government-mandated spin-off from the Rockefellers' Standard Oil Company. It explores for gas and oil as well as distributes natural gas to 1.7 million customers in the Midwest via its local utility subsidiaries. Many other companies utilize the CNG pipelines for transporting their own gas. CNG's network of pipelines is one of the most extensive in the country.

With the coming deregulation of the electric and gas utility industry, it is important to own utilities that not only are solid for the present, but have the potential to compete well in the coming deregulated environment. CNG has that ability. It has set up a subsidiary to market electric power on the wholesale market, and in one year it has come from nowhere to be number four in the industry. The integration of gas and electricity marketing will be a big plus in the future as companies and individuals look to acquire all their energy needs from one source, hopefully at the cheapest possible price.

CNG is also developing new uses for natural gas, such as for cars, trucks, and buses. It has a large fleet of vehicles that run on natural gas. In 1994, 68 million cubic feet of natural gas was used in such vehicles. By 1995 that number had grown to 205 million cubic feet. Natural gas is one of the cleanest burning fuels there is and there should be future markets for this clean fuel in vehicles, utility plants, and elsewhere.

DIVIDEND HISTORY: CONSOLIDATED NATURAL GAS	
1. CONTINUOUS UNINTERRUPTED DIVIDEND PAID SINCE:	1944
2. DIVIDEND PAID IN 1977	$0.58
3. DIVIDEND YIELD IN 1977	8.2%
4. DIVIDEND PAID IN 1997	$1.94
5. 1997 DIVIDEND YIELD BASED ON ORIGINAL INVESTMENT	27%!
6. ANNUAL DIVIDEND GROWTH RATE FOR LAST 10 YEARS	6%
7. ANNUAL DIVIDEND GROWTH SINCE I BOUGHT THIS STOCK	0.40%
8. MY ORIGINAL YIELD	4.93%
9. MY PRESENT YIELD ON ORIGINAL INVESTMENT	6.81%

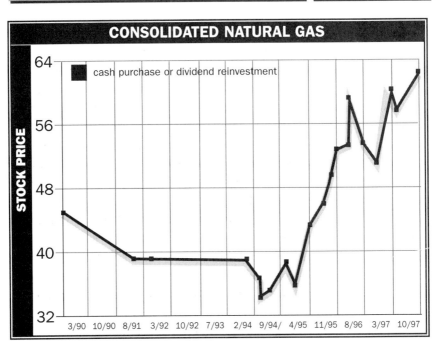

CONSOLIDATED NATURAL GAS

cash purchase or dividend reinvestment

STOCK PRICE

64 — 56 — 48 — 40 — 32

3/90 10/90 8/91 3/92 10/92 7/93 2/94 9/94/ 4/95 11/95 8/96 3/97 10/97

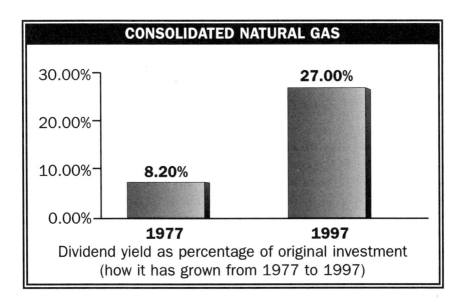

CONSOLIDATED NATURAL GAS

27.00%

8.20%

1977 1997

Dividend yield as percentage of original investment
(how it has grown from 1977 to 1997)

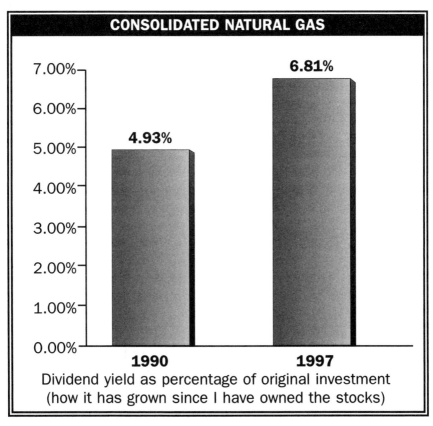

CONSOLIDATED NATURAL GAS

6.81%

4.93%

1990 1997

Dividend yield as percentage of original investment
(how it has grown since I have owned the stocks)

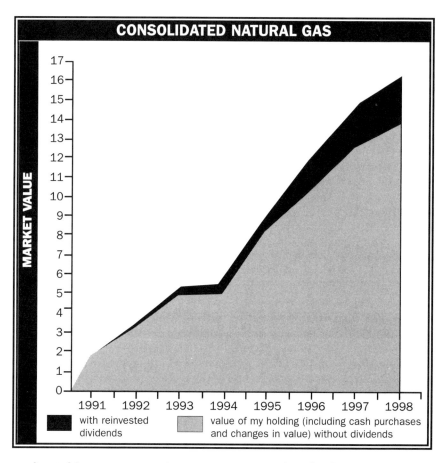

CONSOLIDATED NATURAL GAS

MARKET VALUE

17
16
15
14
13
12
11
10
9
8
7
6
5
4
3
2
1
0

1991 1992 1993 1994 1995 1996 1997 1998

with reinvested dividends

value of my holding (including cash purchases and changes in value) without dividends

A stable, conservative company with which to anchor a portfolio, but with potential for future growth in the deregulated environment.

DOVER CORP.

I came to this stock in a roundabout way. One day I was researching stocks in Value Line in the public library in Dover, Delaware where I did part-time radiology work. I came across a company called the Dover Corporation. I had never heard of the company and was curious if it had anything to do with Dover, Delaware. It didn't. But I looked further and decided it was an outstanding company and one worth including in my portfolio. Dover Corp. is the second largest elevator manufacturer in the

DIVIDEND HISTORY: DOVER CORP.	
1. CONTINUOUS UNINTERRUPTED DIVIDEND PAID SINCE:	1947
2. DIVIDEND PAID IN 1977	$0.05
3. DIVIDEND YIELD IN 1977	2.80%
4. DIVIDEND PAID IN 1997	$0.68
5. 1997 DIVIDEND YIELD BASED ON ORIGINAL INVESTMENT	34%!
6. ANNUAL DIVIDEND GROWTH RATE FOR LAST 10 YEARS	10%
7. ANNUAL DIVIDEND GROWTH SINCE I BOUGHT THIS STOCK	11.30%
8. MY ORIGINAL YIELD	1.73%
9. MY PRESENT YIELD ON ORIGINAL INVESTMENT	2.62%

country, second only to Otis Elevator, a subsidiary of United Technology. But it also is diversified into hundreds of other basic manufacturing areas, from making containers with Coca-Cola's characteristic shape, to gasoline-pump nozzles, to compressors, flow meters, bearings, microwave filters, sucker rods, and valves.

It is diversified into so many different areas that I cannot keep track of them, even when reading the annual report. The products range from those needed in basic smokestack industries to components needed for the highest of high tech. This makes it very resilient to economic factors as some part of the company is always doing something that is still selling well. Elevators are the major part of the company so it has been temporarily hurt in the bottom line during real estate recessions when there is a slowdown in new building construction. Dover picks up some of this slack with its elevator repair and maintenance businesses.

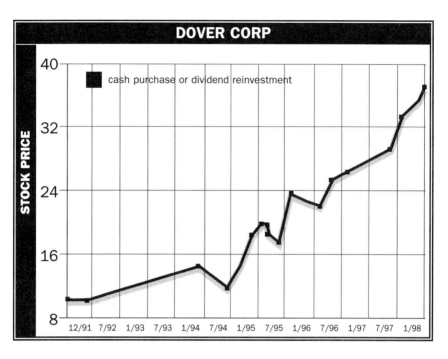

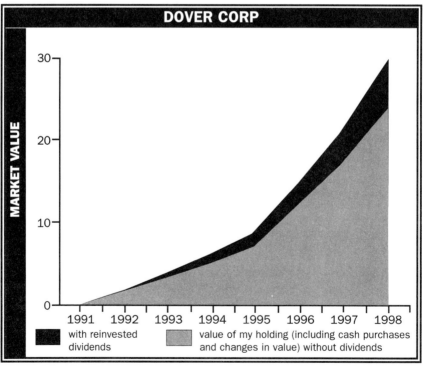

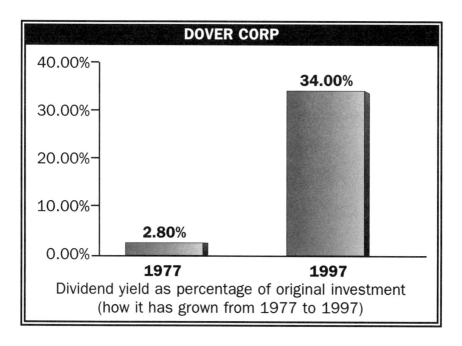

DOVER CORP

40.00%
30.00%
20.00%
10.00%
0.00%

34.00%

2.80%

1977   **1997**

Dividend yield as percentage of original investment
(how it has grown from 1977 to 1997)

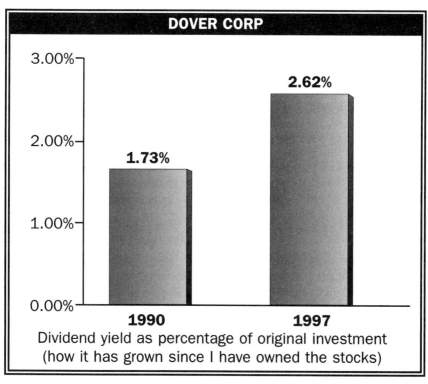

DOVER CORP

3.00%
2.00%
1.00%
0.00%

2.62%

1.73%

1990   **1997**

Dividend yield as percentage of original investment
(how it has grown since I have owned the stocks)

In addition each of the separate areas is run as a separate company. This decentralized management style gives Dover an entrepreneurial bent even though it is so huge. In fact, many of its subsidiary companies were outside companies that were bought out by Dover. Often the original entrepreneur who founded the company was brought on board to continue running it within the Dover family. This individual type of spirit at the various subsidiaries gives Dover many edges over the competition.

I now pay careful attention whenever I ride in an elevator to see who made it. The elevator in the building where my children's pediatrician is located was made by Dover Corp. I always beam proudly when riding up. My wife thinks I am beaming with pride over our *kinderlach*. Little does she know that my heart is glowing with pride at the Dover elevator carrying us up.

Foreign sales account for 20 percent of the total at present.

DUKE ENERGY

Duke Energy is another electric utility that is appropriate to own on its present strengths while at the same time it is better positioned than almost any other utility to deal with the soon-to-be-here deregulated environment. In addition to its core electric utility business in the thriving Piedmont section of the Carolinas, it has many related, well-run, and profitable nonregulated diversified units.

These include Duke Energy Group, Duke Engineering and Services, Duke/Fluor Daniel, Duke Merchandising, DukeNet Communications, Duke Water Operations, Nantahala Power and Light, and others. Included among these subsidiaries are units that design, build, administer, and maintain power plants for other utilities nationwide and overseas, including nuclear power plants. Duke's engineering reputation is world renowned. Duke is involved in a joint venture with Louis Dreyfus Energy to market wholesale electricity and gas nationwide. Louis Dreyfus is the second largest wholesale electric marketer in the country, second only to Enron Corp.

Just last year Duke bought PanEnergy Corp, which distributes 15 percent of the gas in this country, for $7.5 billion, to

DIVIDEND HISTORY: DUKE ENERGY	
1. CONTINUOUS UNINTERRUPTED DIVIDEND PAID SINCE:	1926
2. DIVIDEND PAID IN 1977	$0.77
3. DIVIDEND YIELD IN 1977	7.60%
4. DIVIDEND PAID IN 1997	$2.12
5. 1997 DIVIDEND YIELD BASED ON ORIGINAL INVESTMENT	21%!
6. ANNUAL DIVIDEND GROWTH RATE FOR LAST 10 YEARS	4.5%
7. ANNUAL DIVIDEND GROWTH SINCE I BOUGHT THIS STOCK	have not owned long enough
8. MY ORIGINAL YIELD	4.56%
9. MY PRESENT YIELD ON ORIGINAL INVESTMENT	have not owned long enough to change

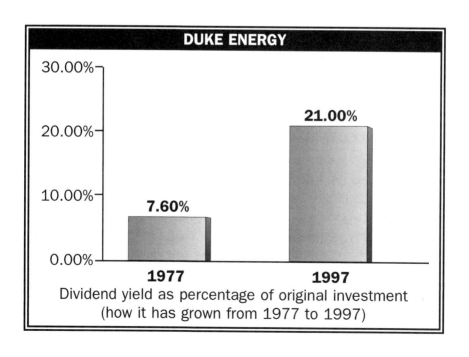

DUKE ENERGY

Dividend yield as percentage of original investment
(how it has grown from 1977 to 1997)

create a combined company worth $23 billion. In the coming deregulated environment, Duke — in combination with Louis Dreyfus Energy and PanEnergy — will be an efficient, low-priced, one-stop shopping energy marketer difficult to match or beat. They just won a contract to provide all of the electricity to the city of Dover, Delaware for the next 10 years. They bested 22 other contenders for the contract.

Duke serves an area with quite a high ratio of industrial customers. This can be a negative as industrial customers may cut back on power usage during a recession. Residential and commercial users usually will not cut back during tough times. A full 33 percent of Duke's customers are industrial users, mostly in textile manufacturing. Duke goes a long way to try and keep its industrial consumers happy. Duke has a special Economic Development Rate which gives a company a 20 percent discount if it will increase its usage by 1 megawatt and either invest an additional $400 in capital upgrades or hire 75 new workers. Modern textile machinery is computer controlled and sensitive. Breaks in current can be very expensive and can greatly disrupt productivity. Therefore Duke works very closely with its larger customers with its Power Quality Process to ensure a steady flow of current, utilizing such advanced tools as SagGen, a computerized sag generator, designed to subject manufacturing equipment to different quality situations before the equipment is placed into service.

GENERAL ELECTRIC

They bring good things to life and to my investment portfolio. Most people know General Electric from its consumer products such as light bulbs and home appliances. Just recently I bought two General Electric telephones. I have owned the stock for many years and until today I didn't know that they also make telephones, plus they own NBC Television and are dominant in plastics, aircraft engines, nuclear and traditional power plants, locomotive engines, and more. They are number 1 or 2 in every business they are in. If not, then they either revamp, sell, or close that business.

DIVIDEND HISTORY: GENERAL ELECTRIC	
1. CONTINUOUS UNINTERRUPTED DIVIDEND PAID SINCE:	1899
2. DIVIDEND PAID IN 1977	$0.22
3. DIVIDEND YIELD IN 1977	3.20%
4. DIVIDEND PAID IN 1997	$2.08
5. 1997 DIVIDEND YIELD BASED ON ORIGINAL INVESTMENT	30%!
6. ANNUAL DIVIDEND GROWTH RATE FOR LAST 10 YEARS	11.50%
7. ANNUAL DIVIDEND GROWTH SINCE I BOUGHT THIS STOCK	13.60%
8. MY ORIGINAL YIELD	2.90%
9. MY PRESENT YIELD ON ORIGINAL INVESTMENT	4.94%

In addition they own GE Capital Services. This financial powerhouse provides a large percentage of GE's revenue and profits. They are into lending, leasing, insurance, credit cards, personal finance and more. GE Capital Services was the provider of the private mortgage insurance (PMI) on our home until we had worked down the principle to the point that we could cancel the PMI.

I also know the company as the world leader in x-ray, CAT scan, ultrasound, and magnetic resonance imaging scanning equipment. I did my radiology training at Albany Medical Center Hospital in upstate New York. There was a major GE plant in nearby Schenectady and we were able to get GE x-ray equipment when it was new and experimental, before it was shipped to other hospitals. We had one of the very first magnetic resonance imaging scanners in all of New York State. Most of the equipment I trained on for years and years was GE.

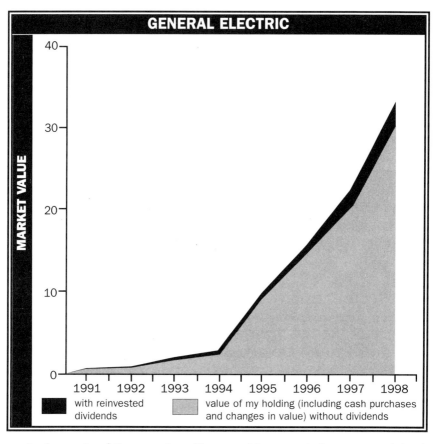

GENERAL ELECTRIC

MARKET VALUE

40 —

30 —

20 —

10 —

0 —

1991 1992 1993 1994 1995 1996 1997 1998

■ with reinvested dividends

▨ value of my holding (including cash purchases and changes in value) without dividends

And speak of the service. If a machine went down, we picked up the phone 24 hours a day, 7 days a week and within an hour there was a technician at our side from GE to help us. Parts were flown in from anywhere in the world if need be. It's not just that we were in Albany near the plant. GE places a large emphasis on providing excellent maintenance and service on its equipment spread around the world, from aircraft engines to power plants to x-ray facilities. The legendary chairman of GE, Jack Welch, has made this a priority at GE, to generate a continuous reliable stream of income to the bottom line from service contracts on the countless billions of dollars of GE equipment scattered world-wide. Technical Services accounts for 10 percent of revenues.

Interestingly enough, Peter Lynch, in his classic work *One Up on Wall Street*, gave General Electric as an example of a stock

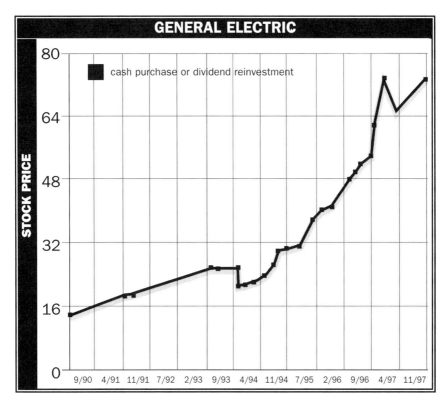

GENERAL ELECTRIC

STOCK PRICE

■ cash purchase or dividend reinvestment

80

64

48

32

16

0

9/90 4/91 11/91 7/92 2/93 9/93 4/94 11/94 7/95 2/96 9/96 4/97 11/97

which may not grow as fast as other stocks. When he wrote his book in 1989 he said that with a market capitalization of $39 billion it was mathematically impossible for GE to double or triple in the near future. Of every dollar spent in America in 1989 a penny was already finding its way to General Electric. Be that as it may, since I first purchased GE on 9/26/90 it has quadrupled in price. GE now stands as the largest capitalized company in the world at $168 billion. The company by itself constitutes 2-4 percent of the S&P 500.

The Wall Street Journal reported just recently that GE is the most profitable company in the country this year, having more net income than any other, a whopping $7.25 billion on revenues of $78 billion. General Electric has never had an operating loss in over 100 years of business. It is the only stock from the original Dow Jones Industrial Index to still be in the index. International business provides 46 percent of sales and 3 percent of sales is spent on research and development.

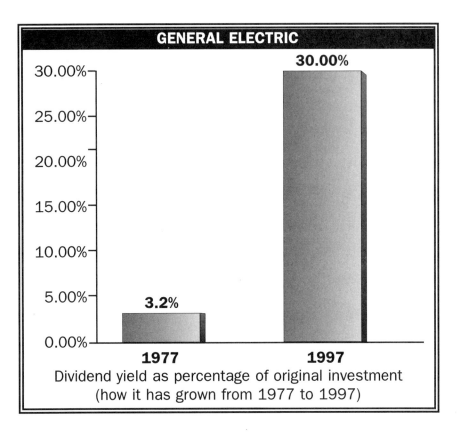

GENERAL ELECTRIC

30.00%

3.2%

1977   1997

Dividend yield as percentage of original investment
(how it has grown from 1977 to 1997)

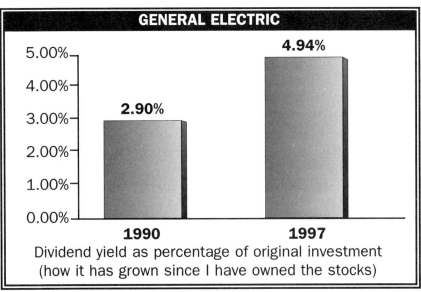

GENERAL ELECTRIC

4.94%

2.90%

1990   1997

Dividend yield as percentage of original investment
(how it has grown since I have owned the stocks)

GILLETTE

This is one stock that I passed up for years, even though Warren Buffett liked it. I thought the dividend rate wasn't high enough (1.4 percent) and that the company had too high a debt ratio (44 percent) when I first considered the stock. But like a good, sharp razor, certain aspects of the Gillette story kept snipping at me.

Firstly, I kept thinking of Mr. Buffett's famous observation: "I go to bed happy at night knowing that hair is growing on billions of male faces and on women's legs around the world. It's more fun that counting sheep." And Gillette does indeed service the vast majority of this market, both here and abroad. In fact, Gillette has anywhere from 70-90 percent of the market in the many countries where it sells its products. Then I noticed that their debt kept dropping (presently only 21 percent) while their dividend kept rising. The original 1.4 percent pay would have been doubled by now to almost 3 percent had I bought the stock eight years ago, plus the stock price has more than doubled and has a long history of steadily rising.

In general, it is not a good idea to buy a stock after it has had a good run-up. But I am in this for the long haul and don't think that over a 30 or 40-year time frame it will matter much when I finally jumped into Gillette. What finally pushed me to buy the stock was an article I had read in *Fortune Magazine* (10/14/96). The article described the high-tech research that Gillette does to keep its leading edge in razors. CEO Albert Zeien believes in true innovation, not, as he puts it, "putting blue dots in the soap power" and calling it new and improved. I had no idea that the phenomenally successful Sensor family of razors took so many years and so much money to develop and that they were so high tech. They cannot be easily duplicated by other companies. Nor did I realize how much men really did prefer them, particulary since I haven't shaved at all for over 20 years.

The straw that broke the camel's back, or in this case the doctor's beard, was the recent acquisition by Gillette of Duracell Battery. Gillette spent a full five years looking carefully and patiently for the right profitable, technologically driven consumer products business to acquire. This is not a company

DIVIDEND HISTORY: GILLETTE	
1. CONTINUOUS UNINTERRUPTED DIVIDEND PAID SINCE:	1906
2. DIVIDEND PAID IN 1977	$0.10
3. DIVIDEND YIELD IN 1977	4.90%
4. DIVIDEND PAID IN 1997	$0.72
5. 1997 DIVIDEND YIELD BASED ON ORIGINAL INVESTMENT	35%!
6. ANNUAL DIVIDEND GROWTH RATE FOR LAST 10 YEARS	12.5%
7. ANNUAL DIVIDEND GROWTH SINCE I BOUGHT THIS STOCK	have not owned long enough
8. MY ORIGINAL YIELD	0.96%
9. MY PRESENT YIELD ON ORIGINAL INVESTMENT	have not owned long enough to change

that blindly diversifies into poorly understood areas. Duracell is the world leader in batteries and Gillette plans to market them in every area of the world where they market razors, which is just about everywhere (foreign business accounts for 70 percent of sales). Both razors and batteries are small point of purchase items which can easily be distributed, marketed, and sold worldwide using the existing Gillette infrastructure. In addition, Duracell gives Gillette new entry into areas of distribution such as home improvement centers where it traditionally did not market razors.

With the addition of Duracell to the Gillette family, the company now stands on six solid legs — wet-shaving razors and blades; Braun electric razors and small appliances; toiletries and cosmetics (Right Guard, Soft & Dri); stationery products (Parker, Paper Mate, and Waterman pens as well as Liquid Paper); Oral-B plain and electric toothbrushes; and Duracell battery products.

I know that I am coming into this one late. Its addition to my

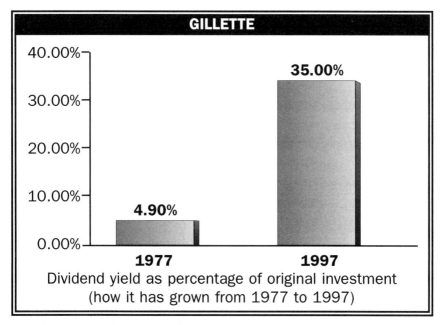

GILLETTE

- 40.00%
- 35.00% (1997)
- 30.00%
- 20.00%
- 10.00%
- 4.90% (1977)
- 0.00%

1977   **1997**

Dividend yield as percentage of original investment
(how it has grown from 1977 to 1997)

portfolio doesn't really influence my present results as I haven't owned it for that long. But in the short time I've owned it, it has already gone up 25 percent. Let's hope that I am on the right track with this one. It's done well for Warren Buffett, I hope it will do well for me, and it most likely will do well for you. And as far as coming in late, remember the famous adage, "The best time to invest in stocks was yesterday. The second best time is today."

HEINZ FOODS

I wanted a food company in my portfolio, because like drugs, like Coke, and like Gillette razors, I figured people will buy ketchup in good times and bad. Among various food processing companies, Heinz appealed to me because I had read an article in *Money Magazine* back in 1990 on how Heinz had had 25 years of uninterrupted increasing profit margins, a feat unmatched in those 25 years by any other corporation in America. I also liked the fact that Heinz had some diversity within food, with domination in various product areas such as ketchup and other condiments, tuna fish (it owns Star-Kist), Ore-Ida frozen potato products, 9-Lives cat food, baby food, as well as the

Weight Watcher's franchise. The very first mass-produced American food certified as kosher by the Orthodox Union almost 100 years ago was good old Heinz baked beans.

A few years after I bought Heinz, my son Elchonan bought 10 shares of Hershey with his *bar-mitzvah* money. I didn't like the fact that Hershey had only chocolate and pasta products, not enough diversity. Well, my son more than doubled his money in Hershey in two years and my Heinz has not quite doubled in almost eight years. But I am not going to go into detail about Hershey here, even though they pay a good dividend. Let my son write his own book. (When I bought Abbott Labs, Elchonan bought Johnson and Johnson, a competing health care company. For various reasons I though Abbott Labs was the better investment of the two. Sure enough his Johnson and Johnson has soundly trounced my Abbott Labs. But hey, I still retired at age 40, so the kid better not gloat too much.)

Heinz has a global reach and foreign sales account for 43 percent of business.

DIVIDEND HISTORY: HEINZ

1. CONTINUOUS UNINTERRUPTED DIVIDEND PAID SINCE:	1911
2. DIVIDEND PAID IN 1977	$0.06
3. DIVIDEND YIELD IN 1977	3.40%
4. DIVIDEND PAID IN 1997	$1.16
5. 1997 DIVIDEND YIELD BASED ON ORIGINAL INVESTMENT	66%!
6. ANNUAL DIVIDEND GROWTH RATE FOR LAST 10 YEARS	14%
7. ANNUAL DIVIDEND GROWTH SINCE I BOUGHT THIS STOCK	11.10%
8. MY ORIGINAL YIELD	3.22%
9. MY PRESENT YIELD ON ORIGINAL INVESTMENT	5.32%

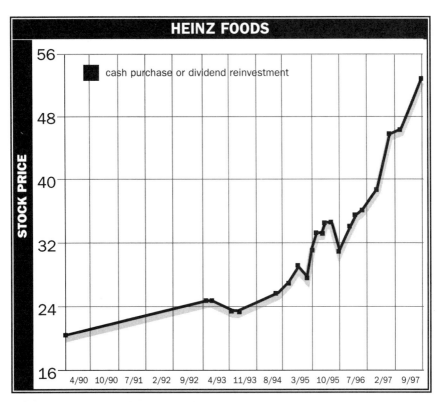

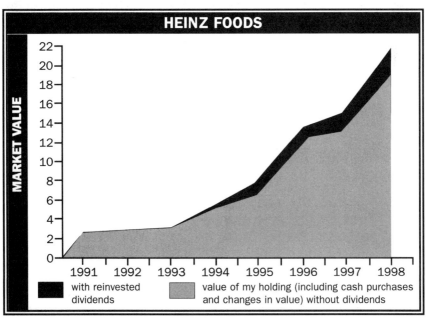

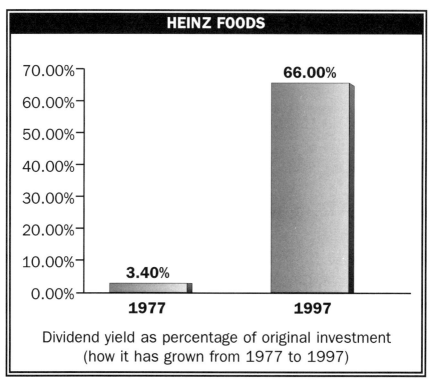

Dividend yield as percentage of original investment
(how it has grown from 1977 to 1997)

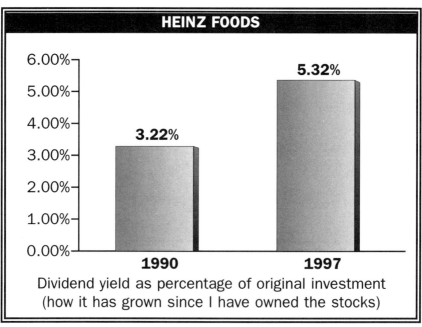

Dividend yield as percentage of original investment
(how it has grown since I have owned the stocks)

HEWLETT PACKARD

There is a wonderful book which was written by company co-founder David Packard before he passed away. It is called *The Hewlett Packard Way* and it is Mr. Packard's inside glimpse of how he and Bill Hewlett founded the company, and indeed all of Silicon Valley, in a small garage behind his home. *The Hewlett Packard Way* is heartwarming for is a story of how the corporation grew based on principles of innovation, helping the community, helping the country, respecting its workers, avoiding layoffs at all costs, giving workers freedom to innovate and freedom to fail. Hewlett Packard is a good corporate citizen and its founders were good American citizens. It is a company that one can own with pride and with the secure knowledge that over the decades to come they will continue to innovate new ideas.

Their first product was an electrical oscillator which was used by Walt Disney in creating the classic cartoon movie *Fantasia*. From there it has been a steady stream of new products from

DIVIDEND HISTORY: HEWLETT PACKARD	
1. CONTINUOUS UNINTERRUPTED DIVIDEND PAID SINCE:	1965
2. DIVIDEND PAID IN 1977	$0.01
3. DIVIDEND YIELD IN 1977	0.3%
4. DIVIDEND PAID IN 1997	$0.48
5. 1997 DIVIDEND YIELD BASED ON ORIGINAL INVESTMENT	14%!
6. ANNUAL DIVIDEND GROWTH RATE FOR LAST 10 YEARS	19%
7. ANNUAL DIVIDEND GROWTH SINCE I BOUGHT THIS STOCK	have not owned long enough
8. MY ORIGINAL YIELD	0.96%
9. MY PRESENT YIELD ON ORIGINAL INVESTMENT	have not owned long enough to change

pocket calculators to computer printers and servers, from electronic measuring devices to medical supplies (many years ago in Israel I used a Hewlett Packard EKG machine and defibrillator). I still recall how the first Hewlett Packard pocket calculators swept the country in 1972. Overnight they virtually eliminated the slide rulers which I and all premed and science students had used for years. From an original price of close to $1000 back in 1972, they have become ubiquitous enough to sell for under $10 today.

The company creates brand-new markets where none existed — like pocket calculators and ink jet and laser printers — and then dominates those areas. Their one weak point used to be marketing. After all, it's a company of engineers. From my NASA days I can assure you that engineers are not an extroverted market-oriented bunch. They used to say that if Hewlett Packard was selling sushi, they would wrap it in plastic and call it "Dead, raw fish." That has changed of late and in addition to unmatched product innovation, Hewlett Packard now markets very well also.

Hewlett Packard, like GE, is heavily into servicing its existing customers. Hewlett Packard also services customers who buy their computers or high-tech equipment from other companies. Service revenues were 14 percent of total last year. Foreign sales are 56 percent and research and development accounts for 7.3 percent of sales.

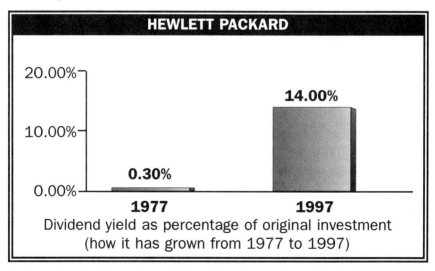

Dividend yield as percentage of original investment
(how it has grown from 1977 to 1997)

ELI LILLY AND CO.

Eli Lilly, like Abbott Labs and Bristol-Myers Squibb, is an old traditional pharmaceutical company. It has been around over a hundred years. It developed the very first injectable insulin in the world and is still the world leader in insulin products. It is also a leader in innovative and new antibiotics (Ceclor, Kefzol, Lorabid, Cefaclor), antidepressants (Prozac) and anti-ulcer medications (Axid).

As I noted before, there are very few drugs in the entire world which sell a billion dollars worth per year. Prozac sells over $2 billion per year. Axid sells $600 million, Cefaclor $750 million, and Humulin insulin $800 million per year. To deal with managed care's inroads on profits, they bought PCS Health Systems, a managed-care pharmaceutical distributor, and Integrated Medical Services, the country's largest communications network for physicians. They also market various veterinary products and medical devices.

DIVIDEND HISTORY: ELI LILLY AND CO.	
1. CONTINUOUS UNINTERRUPTED DIVIDEND PAID SINCE:	1885
2. DIVIDEND PAID IN 1977	$0.16
3. DIVIDEND YIELD IN 1977	2.40%
4. DIVIDEND PAID IN 1997	$1.44
5. 1997 DIVIDEND YIELD BASED ON ORIGINAL INVESTMENT	22%!
6. ANNUAL DIVIDEND GROWTH RATE FOR LAST 10 YEARS	13%
7. ANNUAL DIVIDEND GROWTH SINCE I BOUGHT THIS STOCK	6.50%
8. MY ORIGINAL YIELD	3.06%
9. MY PRESENT YIELD ON ORIGINAL INVESTMENT	5.07%

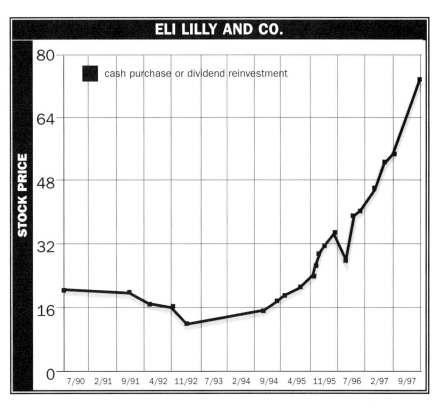

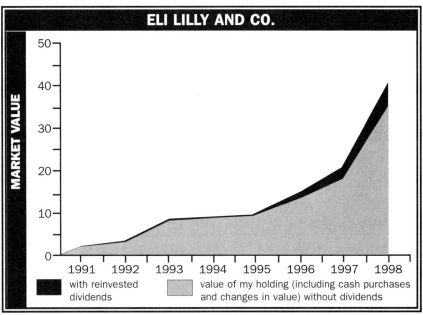

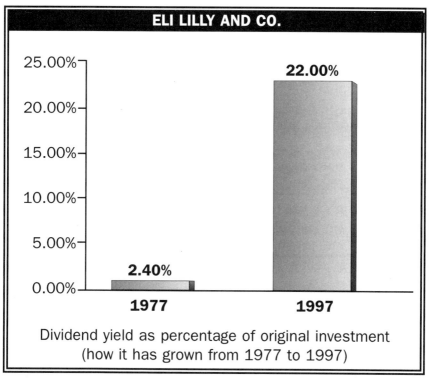

ELI LILLY AND CO.

25.00%
20.00%
15.00%
10.00%
5.00%
0.00%

2.40%
1977

22.00%
1997

Dividend yield as percentage of original investment
(how it has grown from 1977 to 1997)

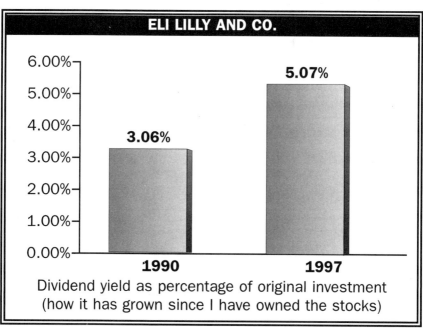

ELI LILLY AND CO.

6.00%
5.00%
4.00%
3.00%
2.00%
1.00%
0.00%

3.06%
1990

5.07%
1997

Dividend yield as percentage of original investment
(how it has grown since I have owned the stocks)

Foreign sales account for 44 percent of total and research and development is 15.4 percent, which is more than $1 billion a year.

On a personal note, my sister helped put her husband through medical school by working as a drug rep for Eli Lilly in the mid 1970s. Lilly is based in Indianapolis and my sister used to get tickets to the Indy 500. But that had no influence whatsoever on my decision to buy the stock. Really.

MERCK

This is my fourth and final drug company. I know. Four drug companies are probably too many for one portfolio but as a physician I am partial to medical companies. In many ways Merck is much like the others: long history of innovative products; good pipeline of new products; inventing whole new classes of medication; paying a rising dividend for decades.

Merck also has a very large veterinary product line. The company is dealing with managed care through the purchase of

DIVIDEND HISTORY: MERCK	
1. CONTINUOUS UNINTERRUPTED DIVIDEND PAID SINCE:	1935
2. DIVIDEND PAID IN 1977	$0.08
3. DIVIDEND YIELD IN 1977	2%
4. DIVIDEND PAID IN 1997	$1.60
5. 1997 DIVIDEND YIELD BASED ON ORIGINAL INVESTMENT	40%!
6. ANNUAL DIVIDEND GROWTH RATE FOR LAST 10 YEARS	21%
7. ANNUAL DIVIDEND GROWTH SINCE I BOUGHT THIS STOCK	14.20%
8. MY ORIGINAL YIELD	2.75%
9. MY PRESENT YIELD ON ORIGINAL INVESTMENT	5.31%

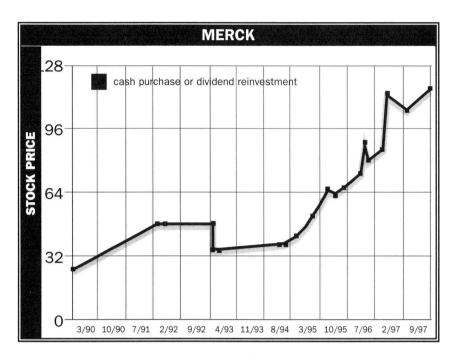

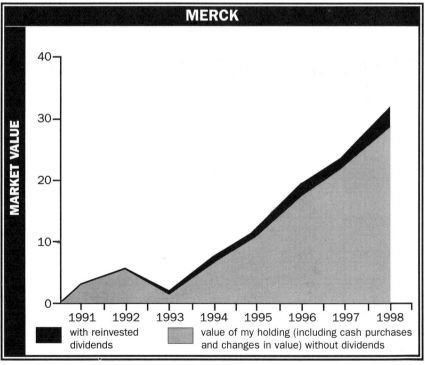

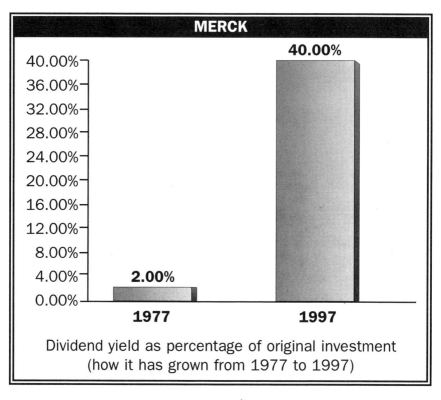

MERCK

Dividend yield as percentage of original investment
(how it has grown from 1977 to 1997)

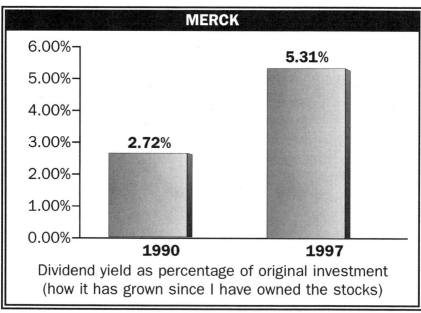

MERCK

Dividend yield as percentage of original investment
(how it has grown since I have owned the stocks)

Medco Containment, a large managed-care distributor of pharmaceuticals. Merck has alliances with DuPont and Johnson and Johnson to develop and market various pharmaceutical products, including over-the-counter medications.

Blockbuster drugs in Merck's present inventory include Vasotec ACE inhibitor for treating hypertension, Mevacor and Zocor for lowering high cholesterol, brand-new Fosamax for treating osteoporosis, and Prilosec and Pepcid for treating ulcers. New drugs are being developed to fight cardiovascular, endocrine, gastrointestinal, infectious, and inflammatory diseases.

Merck is unique among pharmaceutical companies for having a strong presence in vaccinations. It has just developed Varivax vaccine against chicken pox. People may think of chicken pox as a harmless childhood illness but each year 10,000 people are hospitalized due to chicken pox complications and 100 die. When I was a pediatric intern in 1978 a 4-year-old girl was admitted to my service in the middle of the night and died a few hours later of chicken pox pneumonia. We pulled out all stops but nothing we could do could save her. Harmless indeed!

Foreign sales are 30 percent of total, and research and development come in at $1.3 billion, representing 8 percent of sales.

MICROSOFT AND INTEL CORP (THE WINTEL DUOPOLY)

Technically, these technical companies don't belong in this book or in my portfolio. Microsoft pays no dividend and Intel just recently started paying a minuscule, though rapidly growing, dividend. This violates my cardinal rule of only owning companies which have paid a steadily increasing dividend for endless years on end. But owning Hewlett Packard perked my interest in technology companies. Also, we recently bought our first home computer (albeit a Macintosh) which has increased my knowledge of the whole computer industry.

We all have a little daring in us. I have so many conservative dividend paying investments that I figured a little extra risk wouldn't hurt. Besides, these two high-tech companies are a very small percent of my overall portfolio. My wife knew a lot about computers from her days working in Information Services at Johns Hopkins Hospital in Baltimore before our marriage. She recommended Microsoft even though I was leaning toward Novell (a networking leader). So I passed on Novell and bought Microsoft. Well, Microsoft has more than septupled for us in less than five years while Novell went down 60 percent in the same time period. We jointly decided on Intel and it has more than doubled in less than 18 months!

Even though these returns are somewhat eye popping, I still worry over these stocks. I am sure that they can go down just as rapidly as they went up, with no dividend to prop them up during a market decline. They are complex companies to understand in a complex and rapidly changing industry. I can predict that Coke or Heinz or Gillette will more or less do the same things for the next 100 years that they have done for the past 100 years. Coke is Coke, ketchup is ketchup, and shaving is shaving, more or less. But Microsoft or Intel? Their industries are changing so rapidly that I do not believe that even Microsoft Chairman Bill Gates or Intel Chairman Andy Grove themselves have any idea what it is they will have to be inventing and marketing 10 years from now to survive. Witness Bill Gates' recent, rapid, and total turnaround from no internet presence to a massive internet emphasis throughout the company.

Be that as it may, if you want to own a high-tech company, these are two solid ones. Microsoft is the largest software company in the word and dominates operating systems, applications, and networking software, and probably will soon dominate the internet. Ninety percent of computers in the world are using Microsoft software.

Intel dominates the market for PC microprocessors and other solid-state products such as flash memory found in cellular phones. They hold the same 90 percent share of the market as Microsoft. The barriers of entry for any competitor are very high if not impregnable. Chip-production factories cost billions to build. Intel has spent $10 billion since 1991 and now has 12 chip-production factories scattered worldwide. Recently *The*

Wall Street Journal reported that Intel is preparing to spend an eye popping $4.5 billion this coming year on capital projects, including a new plant in Israel.

One final note on Intel's dividend. It just started paying a dividend in 1992 but the dividend has already quadrupled. Just recently *The Wall Street Journal* reported that Intel is poised to split its stock 2:1 and double the dividend. That would make an eight-fold rise since 1992. At that rate, a minuscule dividend may actually become very significant quite soon. I will patiently wait and see.

MINNESOTA MINING AND MANUFACTURING (3M)

Like GE and Hewlett Packard, 3M is a well-diversified and innovative company. It prides itself on bringing in 30 percent of profits from products developed in the last five years. Each 3M worker is allowed to spend 15 percent of his corporate time working on projects outside his main area of assignment. It is through this corporate encouragement that Post-It Notes were invented. A 3M-worker needed a way to keep little markers in his hymnal during choir practice. 3M's thrust had always been on stronger adhesives. Well, this guy went the other way and started working on weaker adhesives. The rest is history. Post-It Notes are one of the greatest corporate success stories of all time.

A recent innovation is a new breakthrough in material sciences — microreplication. This is the creation of a precise replicating 3D pattern on plastic films and other surfaces. It can be used in abrasives (for finely grinding golf clubs or metal orthopedic implants), reflecting materials (on highways, safety vests, graphics), to make counterfeit-proof plastic ID badges, and even to make a better computer mousepad. 3M expects this new technology to contribute $1 billion in sales by the year 2000.

All of 3M's divisions work fluidly with one another to lead to the greatest innovation, development, and marketing of new products. Products include adhesive tapes, roofing materials, fire-retardant materials, insulating materials

DIVIDEND HISTORY: 3M	
1. CONTINUOUS UNINTERRUPTED DIVIDEND PAID SINCE:	1916
2. DIVIDEND PAID IN 1977	$0.37
3. DIVIDEND YIELD IN 1977	2.40%
4. DIVIDEND PAID IN 1997	$1.96
5. 1997 DIVIDEND YIELD BASED ON ORIGINAL INVESTMENT	13%!
6. ANNUAL DIVIDEND GROWTH RATE FOR LAST 10 YEARS	7.50%
7. ANNUAL DIVIDEND GROWTH SINCE I BOUGHT THIS STOCK	4.30%
8. ORIGINAL YIELD	3.35%
9. MY PRESENT YIELD ON ORIGINAL INVESTMENT	4.19%

(Thinsulate), Scotchgard fabric and carpet protectors, O-Cell-O sponges, medical products such as patches to deliver medications through the skin, graphic arts and much, much more.

3M is a good corporate citizen and is good to its employees. 3M is leading the fight against the often shoddy medical care provided by managed care. Along with several other large corporations based in Minneapolis-St. Paul, such as Dayton-Hudson, Cargill, General Mills and Honeywell, they are rejecting the HMO middlemen who skim hundreds of millions of dollars of health-care dollars from the patients and give it to HMO management and shareholders. 3M and these other companies are self-insuring and thereby are these hundreds of millions of dollars back to work for their employees, if they should be ill and need it. *The Wall Street Journal* and *Business Week* have recently written this up as a possible model for solving managed-care problems in this country.

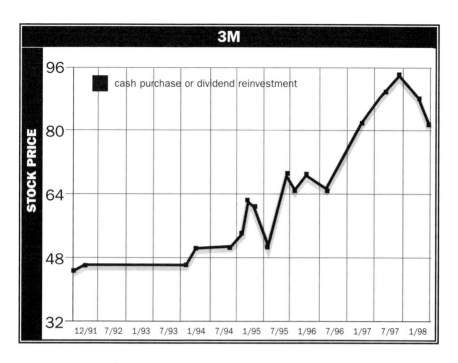

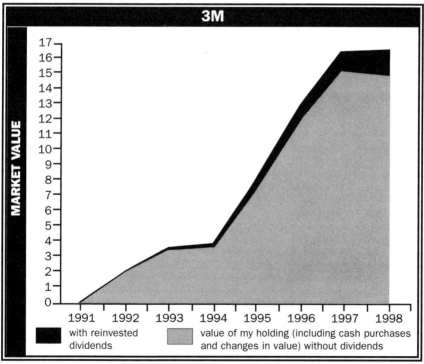

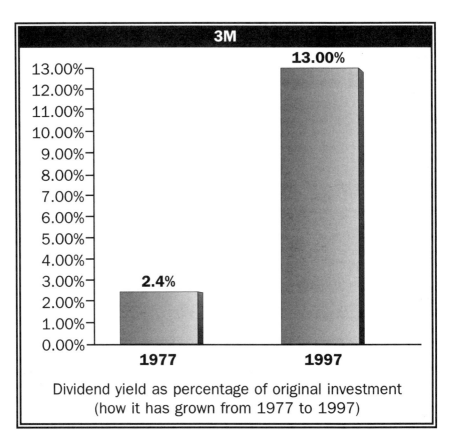

Dividend yield as percentage of original investment
(how it has grown from 1977 to 1997)

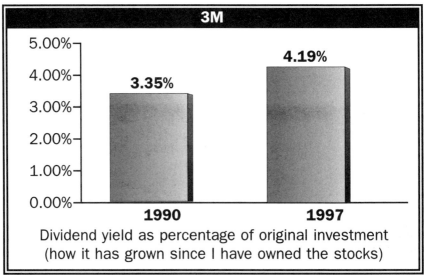

Dividend yield as percentage of original investment
(how it has grown since I have owned the stocks)

Foreign sales account for 54 percent of total and research and development 6.5 percent.

PNC BANK CORP.

PNC Bank Corp. is a large mid-Atlantic bank with a presence in several states including Pennsylvania, New Jersey, Ohio, and Delaware. I have had a banking relationship with PNC for many years. I used to work in Dover, Delaware and did my banking at the Bank of Delaware. The Bank of Delaware was subsequently bought out by PNC, which is based in Pittsburgh. I had been a very satisfied customer with Bank of Delaware and continue to this day as a satisfied customer with PNC Bank.

The majority of my pension, and all of the stocks which I own, are held for me at PNC Securities, a discount broker associated with the bank. If a customer needs more hand-holding, they offer fuller service as well. Our wills and trusts are domiciled at PNC Bank. I have also been in their Private Banking Group, an area of personalized service which they pioneered long before many of the bigger New York banks, with their unique PNC Personal Asset Manager Account. Over the years I have been a loan client as well. PNC can almost be thought of as a diversified financial services company as opposed to a bank, as they offer such high-quality innovative products in so many financial areas.

In all areas I was impressed with their service and bought their stock after researching my favorite bank in Value Line and discovering that the fundamentals matched their excellent service. They are a strong bank financially and have sidestepped many of the danger areas of recent years such as foreign loans and poor real estate loans. Their overhead is one of the lowest in the nation. Their nonperforming loans are small at .88 percent of total assets and their coverage is good.Their dividend has been continually paid and growing since 1865.

Just this year PNC was awarded an exclusive contract by AAA of America to exclusively market banking products to their 34 million customers nationwide. The average AAA member household has 14 percent higher household income than the rest of the country. These households represent $750 billion of deposits and $500 billion in loans. The marketing to

DIVIDEND HISTORY: PNC BANK CORP.	
1. CONTINUOUS UNINTERRUPTED DIVIDEND PAID SINCE:	1865
2. DIVIDEND PAID IN 1977	$0.23
3. DIVIDEND YIELD IN 1977	5.10%
4. DIVIDEND PAID IN 1997	$1.48
5. 1997 DIVIDEND YIELD BASED ON ORIGINAL INVESTMENT	33%!
6. ANNUAL DIVIDEND GROWTH RATE FOR LAST 10 YEARS	8.50%
7. ANNUAL DIVIDEND GROWTH SINCE I BOUGHT THIS STOCK	5.10%
8. MY ORIGINAL YIELD	5.50%
9. MY PRESENT YIELD ON ORIGINAL INVESTMENT	7.62%

this unique group of new customers will be by mail, phone, and even fax. PNC will potentially pick up a lot of new business without the expense of building and maintaining new branches.

This is also one of my favorite stocks for another reason. I bought a large position in the stock only to see Warren Buffett buy 6 percent of the company a week later. This is the one and only time I ever have, and probably ever will, buy a stock ahead of Warren Buffett. It was good for a quick boost in the stock price. But even more so it was good for a quick boost to my ego. After buying the stock Mr. Buffett was quoted in the media saying all sorts of wonderful things about PNC Bank. I had been saying the same things for weeks to my wife as I touted the stock to her. I like to think that Mr. Buffett found out I had bought a large amount of PNC Bank stock and that is the reason he bought in. When I met him at the Coca-Cola shareholders' meeting in 1994 I was tempted to ask him if I had influenced his decision to buy. My son was

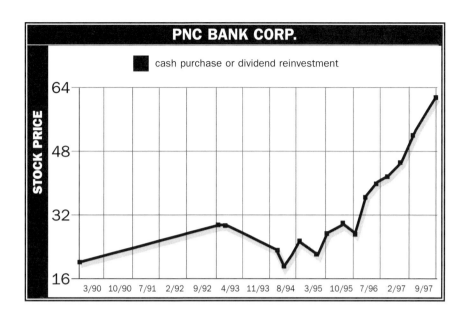

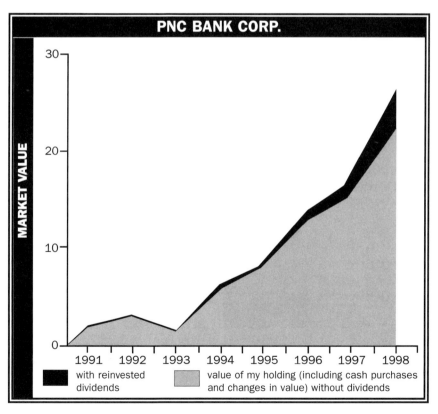

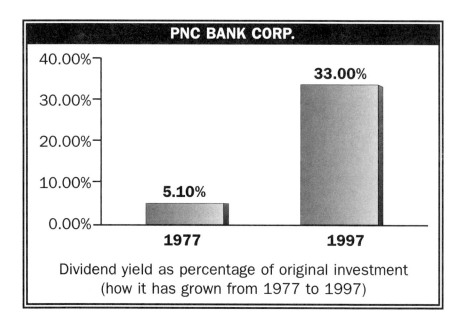

PNC BANK CORP.

5.10% (1977), 33.00% (1997)

Dividend yield as percentage of original investment
(how it has grown from 1977 to 1997)

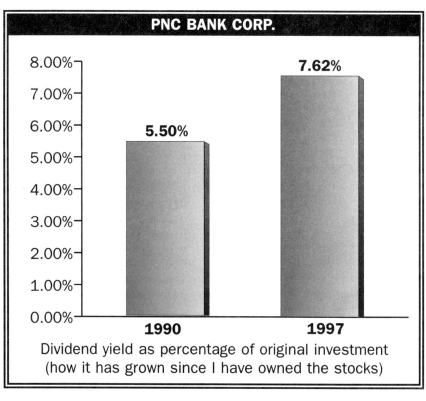

PNC BANK CORP.

5.50% (1990), 7.62% (1997)

Dividend yield as percentage of original investment
(how it has grown since I have owned the stocks)

wise enough to tell me to ask for an autographed annual report instead. I guess it will be Warren's little secret and mine.

TECO ENERGY (TAMPA ELECTRIC)

An excellent electric utility in a growing area of northern Florida, a pro-utility state. It is a good investment on its present merits and it should do well in the coming deregulated environment. It has major well-run diversified efforts which bring in unregulated revenue. Many other utilities diversified 10 years ago into poorly understood unrelated businesses, often with disastrous results including bankruptcy. TECO only runs a diversified business if it relates well to the core business of electric power generation.

TECO mines and transport nonpolluting low-sulfur coal. It burns this coal in its own power plants as well as selling it to other utilities which must comply with federal regulations on coal sulfur emissions. It builds independent power plants (IPP's) in America and in foreign countries, such as Guatemala. It runs a very profitable gas-exploration subsidiary in Alabama. It has a low industrial user base (16 percent) and a high residential and commercial base (76 percent combined). These are customers who will use electricity even during a recession.

Tampa Electric generates its electricity solely through the burning of coal. This could be a negative if the coal were the high-sulfur polluting type. However TECO exclusively uses low-sulfur nonpolluting coal. Its generating plants are so environmentally friendly that Secretary of Energy Hazel O'Leary dedicated the new Tampa Electric Polk Power Plant and praised TECO for its clean use of coal.

I read an article last year in *Forbes Magazine* about the lack of good software to control and track electric usage at large companies, institutes, universities, etc. These bulk users of electricity would like to be able to tell from an electric bill how much energy was used by each building, each office in a building, each classroom, etc. They want to be able to automatically control usage and have smart systems that talk back and forth with the utility electronically, to adjust usage during different periods of

DIVIDEND HISTORY: TECO ENERGY	
1. CONTINUOUS UNINTERRUPTED DIVIDEND PAID SINCE:	1900
2. DIVIDEND PAID IN 1977	$0.28
3. DIVIDEND YIELD IN 1977	6.10%
4. DIVIDEND PAID IN 1997	$1.12
5. 1997 DIVIDEND YIELD BASED ON ORIGINAL INVESTMENT	24%!
6. ANNUAL DIVIDEND GROWTH RATE FOR LAST 10 YEARS	6.50%
7. ANNUAL DIVIDEND GROWTH SINCE I BOUGHT THIS STOCK	4.90%
8. MY ORIGINAL YIELD	4.74%
9. MY PRESENT YIELD ON ORIGINAL INVESTMENT	7.22%

varying demand. Many companies have tried to design the software and all have failed for various reasons.

So I wrote a letter to Mr. James F. Orr, the president and CEO of Cincinnati Bell Information Services (CBIS)(see the stock above under Cincinnati Bell), asking if perhaps CBIS could get into this potentially lucrative field. As you read above, CBIS has tremendous expertise in cellular phone and cable TV billing, which was one of the reasons I had bought the stock. Why not develop and market utility-billing software? The president wrote me back a warm personal letter explaining that CBIS had actually considered my idea in the past but then decided to stick to billing areas specifically in telecommunications.

Oh well, at least I had tried to influence a major corporation of which I am a stockholder. The effort was fun and it made me feel like a good, involved shareholder. Well, just a few weeks later my 1995 annual report for TECO Energy arrived and lo and behold, it was touting a brand new area of diversification.

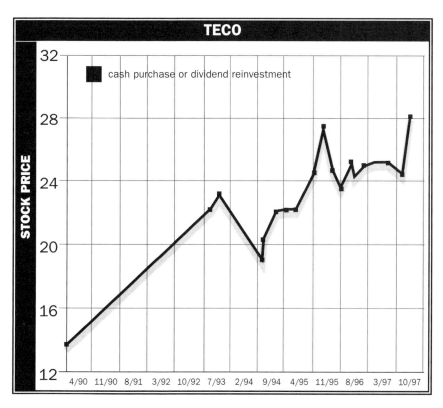

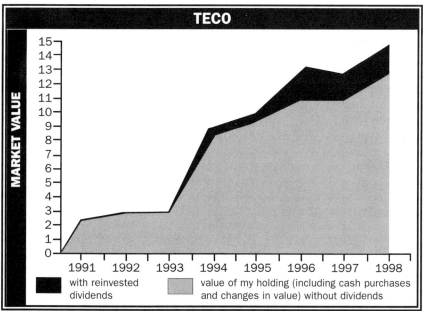

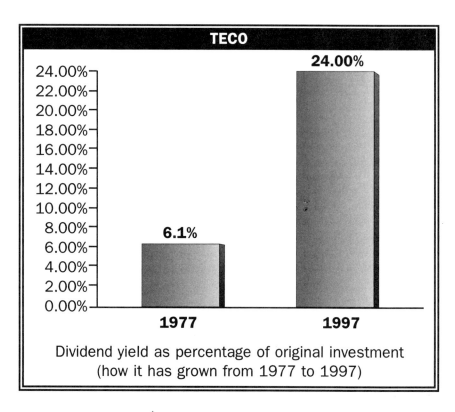

TECO

24.00%

Dividend yield as percentage of original investment
(how it has grown from 1977 to 1997)

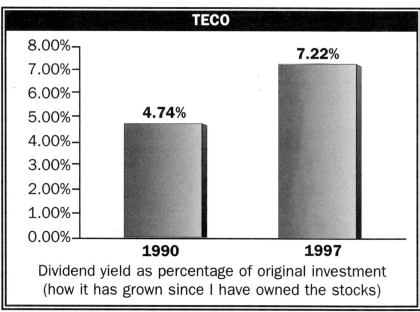

TECO

Dividend yield as percentage of original investment
(how it has grown since I have owned the stocks)

TECO Energy had set up a subsidiary called TeCom and it was developing and marketing the very software I had suggested to CBIS and which *Forbes* magazine had said was desperately needed by the utilities of America for future competition. So one of my stocks didn't go for it, but TECO Energy already had.

The new software is called the Interlane interactive system. Just recently I read a story from Reuter's on the internet describing how Idaho Power Company, a major northwest electric utility, is testing the Interlane system for possible use. This may be an area of great revenue in the future. Interestingly enough, I recently found out that another of my utilities (Wisconsin Energy) is developing similar software in conjunction with Ameritech (the Wisconsin Baby Bell).

WACHOVIA BANK

A well-run, financially sound bank in a thriving area stretching

DIVIDEND HISTORY: WACHOVIA BANK	
1. CONTINUOUS UNINTERRUPTED DIVIDEND PAID SINCE:	1936
2. DIVIDEND PAID IN 1977	$0.13
3. DIVIDEND YIELD IN 1977	2.90%
4. DIVIDEND PAID IN 1997	$1.60
5. 1997 DIVIDEND YIELD BASED ON ORIGINAL INVESTMENT	36%!
6. ANNUAL DIVIDEND GROWTH RATE FOR LAST 10 YEARS	13%
7. ANNUAL DIVIDEND GROWTH SINCE I BOUGHT THIS STOCK	11%
8. MY ORIGINAL YIELD	3.57%
9. MY PRESENT YIELD ON ORIGINAL INVESTMENT	5.28%

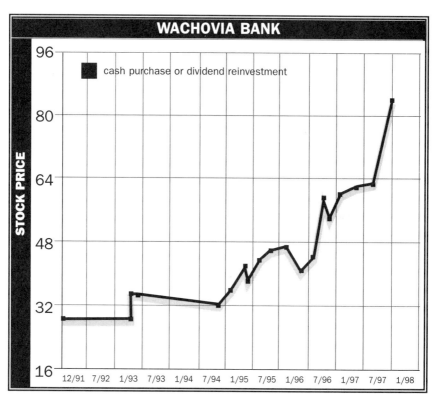

WACHOVIA BANK

■ cash purchase or dividend reinvestment

STOCK PRICE

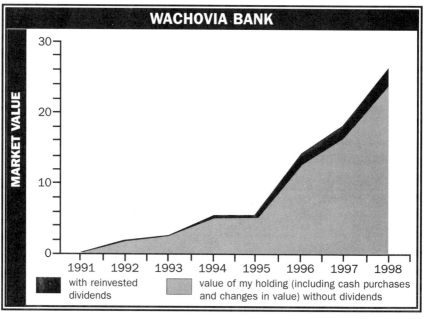

WACHOVIA BANK

MARKET VALUE

with reinvested dividends

value of my holding (including cash purchases and changes in value) without dividends

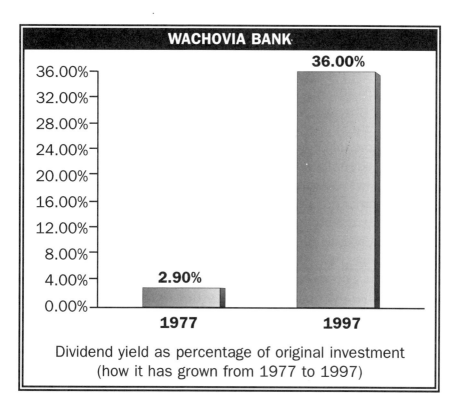

WACHOVIA BANK

Dividend yield as percentage of original investment
(how it has grown from 1977 to 1997)

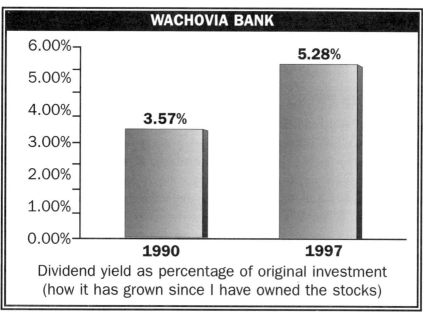

WACHOVIA BANK

Dividend yield as percentage of original investment
(how it has grown since I have owned the stocks)

from the Carolinas to Atlanta, Georgia. Actually, one of the strongest banks in the country. Its nonperforming loan ratio in 1995 was .24 percent, the lowest of the 25 largest banks in the country. This small amount of nonperforming loans is amply covered with reserves of over 763 percent, the second highest coverage rate in the country.

I had personal experience with the bank, as they serviced my medical student loans. I had always felt they gave good service and they always seemed to be one step ahead technologically. My research of the stock in Value Line was extremely favorable.

My father managed some of my student loans for me years ago while I was living in *Eretz Israel* for a few years. He told me that he always enjoyed talking with the friendly southerners who handled his phone calls. My father has lived in New York City his whole life and he is used to a certain toughness in everyone from taxi drivers to bank tellers. I think he was really taken with the pleasant, polite, and, well, "Southerners" at Wachovia. A Carolina accent is simply softer and nicer than a Brooklyn one. When I lived overseas, certain questions arose as to student deferments and other issues concerning my loans. I've always wondered if my father thought of some of these questions just to have an excuse to call the friendly people at Wachovia. I think he was really disappointed when Wachovia finally sold my loans to a processor based in Minnesota.

WISCONSIN ENERGY

Last but not least, my third electric utility. Actually, maybe it is last as well as least, as Wisconsin Energy has been one of my poorer performers. At least on capital gains alone. But when combined with dividends it has actually done quite well.

It is a well-run utility in Wisconsin. It has solid financial fundamentals. It has a well-diversified fuel mix including coal (65 percent), nuclear (25 percent), hydroelectric and gas (1 percent), and purchased power (8 percent). Its nuclear power plants are just about the best run in the country, right up there with Duke Power (see above). The regulatory environment in Wisconsin is above average and is pro-utility. It has a small, but

DIVIDEND HISTORY: WISCONSIN ENERGY	
1. CONTINUOUS UNINTERRUPTED DIVIDEND PAID SINCE:	1939
2. DIVIDEND PAID IN 1977	$0.44
3. DIVIDEND YIELD IN 1977	7.10%
4. DIVIDEND PAID IN 1997	$1.52
5. 1997 DIVIDEND YIELD BASED ON ORIGINAL INVESTMENT	25%!
6. ANNUAL DIVIDEND GROWTH RATE FOR LAST 10 YEARS	6.50%
7. ANNUAL DIVIDEND GROWTH SINCE I BOUGHT THIS STOCK	4.20%
8. MY ORIGINAL YIELD	5.21%
9. MY PRESENT YIELD ON ORIGINAL INVESTMENT	7.44%

well-run diversification program in real estate, recycling, and some other areas. It has initiated a venture with Ameritech (the local Baby Bell) to wire up "smart" houses that can communicate with the utility company electronically to more efficiently control electric usage. It also markets natural gas within its service area, which includes Milwaukee.

By the way, my children have grandparents who live near Milwaukee. Now, at home, in order to help my early retirement, the kids are encouraged to turn off unneeded lights and take other measures to lower our utility bills. However, when they visit Grandma and Grandpa in Wisconsin I've tried to get them to sneak on all the lights they can, take long hot showers, or do whatever else they can do to increase their grandparents' energy bill. Figure it could help my stock. Hey! There's more than one way to skin a cat (or make an investment grow).

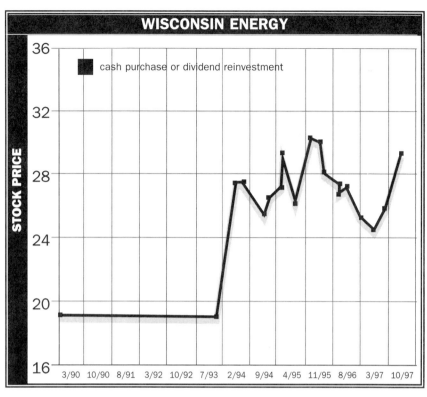

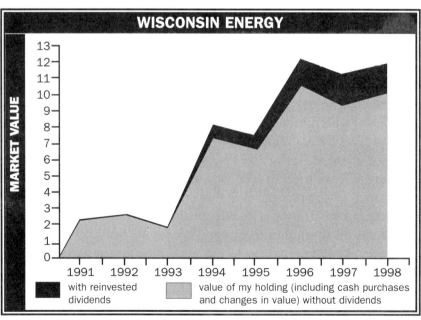

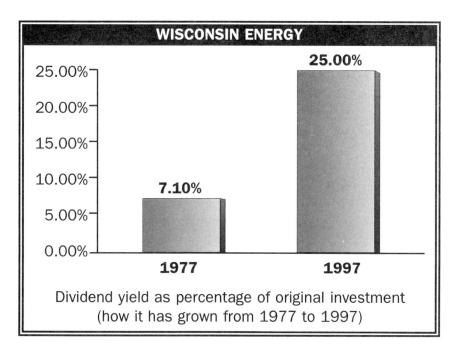

Dividend yield as percentage of original investment
(how it has grown from 1977 to 1997)

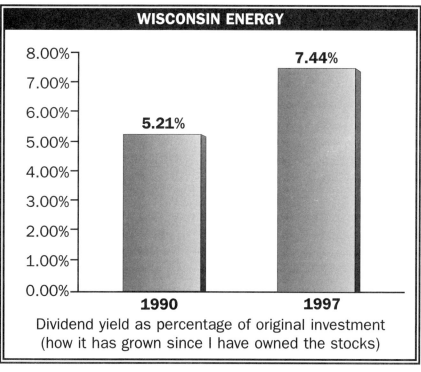

Dividend yield as percentage of original investment
(how it has grown since I have owned the stocks)

CONCLUDING THOUGHTS

hope that from reading this book you have obtained several things. On a practical level I hope that you have acquired an appreciation for the following investing truths:

1) A well-diversified portfolio containing common stocks of name-brand companies can provide excellent long-term growth.

2) Individuals can achieve returns on their stocks which match and beat the professional mutual fund managers.

3) Reinvested dividends are crucial to long-term success in stock investing.

An adequate amount of money may be a prerequisite to attaining some dreams but it is only a means to an end. Money is not the end goal in and of itself. Learning and teaching Torah and doing *mitzvos* is the end goal.

Remember that living rich doesn't mean that you are rich. Living frugally is what can help the average person achieve financial security. Richness involves more than having money. It involves family, spiritual values, and helping others.

APPENDIX 1
SUGGESTED READING LIST

BOOKS

The books listed below are helpful references which discuss the value of patient long-term investing in conservative stocks, how to pick stocks, and the value of dividends. The two books by Charles B. Carlson (*Buying Stocks Without a Broker* and *No Load Stocks*) are especially helpful as they detail how to buy stocks directly from companies without any commissions and how to enroll in dividend reinvestment programs. For people with smaller amounts to invest, these two books are invaluable.

The 100 Best Stocks to Own in America by Gene Walden
　　Useful information on many excellent stocks.

The Beardstown Ladies Common Sense Investment Guide by the Beardstown Ladies Investment Club with Leslie Whitaker

Practical investment advice concerning stock selection by a women's group who averaged 23.4 percent returns.

Beating the Street by Peter Lynch
Classic book on fundamentals of stock selection. Emphasizes how the common man can beat the Wall Street professionals with a little careful research and patience (also authored *One Up on Wall Street*, see below).

Buying Stocks Without a Broker by Charles B. Carlson
Information on Dividend Reinvestment Programs offered by some of America's finest companies (also authored *No Load Stocks*, see below).

Dividends Don't Lie by Geraldine Weiss and Janet Lowe
Importance of dividends as well as a unique system for buying and selling stocks based on the dividend yield.

The Dividend Rich Investor by Joseph Tigue and Joseph Lisanti
Everything you would every want to know about the importance of dividends. Many helpful charts.

The Millionaire Next Door by Thomas J. Stanley and William D. Danko
The average millionaire would surprise you. You could be the next one.

The Motley Fool Investment Guide by David and Tom Gardner
How to get high returns by buying the stocks from the Dow Jones Industrial Index with the highest dividend yields each January.

No Load Stocks by Charles B. Carlson
Buying stocks directly from some of America's finest companies (see above, *Buying Stocks Without a Broker*).

One Up On Wall Street by Peter Lynch
Classic book on fundamentals of stock selection. Emphasizes how the common man can beat the Wall Street professionals with a little careful research and patience (see above, *Beating the Street*).

Starting Small, Investing Smart by Don Nichols
> This is the first investment book I ever read. It is an excellent primer on conservatively investing $5 or $5000 for the long term.

Stocks for the Long Run by Jeremy J. Siegel
> Excellent book on stocks in general with some discussion of dividends.

The Warren Buffett Way by Robert G. Hagstrom, Jr.
> Fundamentals of stock selection showing that billionaires are not the only ones who can analyze and pick stocks.

The Wealthy Barber by David Chilton
> Homespun conservative investment advice.

Whiz Kid of Wall Street's Investment Guide by Matt Seto
> A 17-year-old who has achieved 34 percent returns. Practical stock-picking advice.

REFERENCE VOLUMES

The following reference works are available in public libraries and are very helpful for researching historical data on stocks.

Value Line Investment Survey — gives 15 years of historical data on stocks, descriptions of each company, as well as detailed information about whole segments of industry.

Standard & Poors Research Reports — gives 10 years of historical data on stocks as well as descriptions of each company.

APPENDIX 2
GETTING STARTED

Direct-buy and dividend-reinvestment programs

Below is a table which will be helpful for someone who wants to set up a steady investment program directly from the companies which are described in this book. There are "No-Load Stock Programs" which allow you to steadily buy shares directly from the companies without any brokerage commissions. They will even sell you fractional shares (some for as little as $10 at a time). These are excellent programs for accumulating wealth slowly and steadily with small or large amounts of money. In addition there are DRIPS (Dividend Reinvestment Programs) in which the companies continually reinvest your dividends for free in additional fractional shares (even if the divided is only pennies). Over time these can add up to huge amounts of wealth. See Appendix 1 for two books by Charles B. Carlson (*Buying Stocks Without a Broker* and *No Load Stocks*) which give similar information for hundreds of other companies. The latter book lists companies which enable you to even buy your very first share from them commission-free. At present, however, most companies require you to buy your first share from a broker (and pay the commission) and then allow you to continually add extra shares for the rest of your life commission free directly from the company.

ABBOTT LABS

617-575-2900 • 708-937-3923
847-937-7300 • 847-937-6100

Amounts allowed: $10-$10,000 per quarter

AMERICAN WATER WORKS

609-346-8200 • 617-575-3100 • 800-736-3001

Amounts allowed: 5% discount on reinv. divs.

BOEING

800-733–5001 • 206-655-1990 • 206-655-2121

Call for current guidelines

BRISTOL-MYERS SQUIBB

212-546-4000 • 800-356-2026

Amounts allowed:
$10-$2500 per month (must already own 50 shares)

CINCINNATI BELL

800-321-1355 • 513-397-7877 • 800-542-7792

Amounts allowed: $5,000 per month

COCA-COLA

404-676-2777 • 800-446-2617 • 888-COKESHR

Amounts allowed: $10-$60,000 per year

CONSOLIDATED NATURAL GAS

412-227-1125 • 412-227-1485
800-542-7792 • 216-813-5745

Amounts allowed: $25-$5,000 per quarter

DUKE POWER

800-488-3853 • 704-382-3853

Amounts allowed: $25 (less than $6,000 per quarter)

GENERAL ELECTRIC

203-373-2816 • 203-326-4040
800-786-2543 • 713-651-5065

Amounts allowed: $10-$10,000 per month

GILLETTE

800-643-6989 • 617-575-3170 • 617-421-7000

Amounts allowed: $10-$10,000 per month

HEINZ

412-236-8000 • 412-456-5700 • 800-253-3399

Amounts allowed: $25-$1,000 per month

HEWLETT PACKARD

800-286-5977 • 312-461-4061

Amounts allowed: call for current guidelines

INTEL

312-461-5545

Amounts allowed: call for current guidelines

ELI LILLY

800-833-8699

Amounts allowed: $25-$50,000 per year

MERCK

908-594-6627 • 800-613-2104

Amounts allowed: $25-$5,000 per quarter

3M

612-450-4064 • 612-733-1110 • 800-522-3767

Amounts allowed: $25-$10,000 per quarter

PNC BANK

800-843-2206 • 800-982-7652

Amounts allowed: $50-$1,000 per month

TAMPA ELECTRIC

800-650-9222 • 813-228-4111

Amounts allowed: call for current guidelines

WACHOVIA BANK

910-732-5787 • 800-633-4236

Amounts allowed: $20-$2,000 per month

WISCONSIN ENERGY

800-558-9663

Amounts allowed: $25-$3,000 per month

Below are several companies which allow you to buy your very first share directly from them. Therefore, you never have to use a broker or pay any commissions. Additional programs are constantly being added, so inquire at the phone numbers above.

AMERICAN WATER WORKS

Minimum investment: $100

DUKE POWER

Minimum investment: $25 per quarter

GILLETTE

Minimum investment: Call for current guidelines

WISCONSIN ENERGY

Minimum investment: $25

SUMMARY OF GETTING STARTED

1. Call the phone number of the company whose stock you wish to purchase and find out how many shares you need in order to enroll in their DRIP program. For example Coke requires only 1 share, but Hewlett Packard requires that you start with 10 shares.
2. If the company lets you purchase your first share from them, fine. If not, then call any reputable stock broker of your choice and buy the shares you need. If you so desire, you can shop around for the cheapest commission. However, being this is the only time you will pay a commission, hopefully for many decades, do not worry so much about this one-time fee.
3. VERY, VERY IMPORTANT! Tell your broker to register the shares in your (or your child's) name as the SHAREHOLDER OF RECORD. Have him mail you the stock certificate so that you physically possess it. DO NOT have the shares registered into your regular brokerage account or in STREET NAME. If you do that, then you cannot enroll in the company DRIP program.
4. Once you have the stock certificate in your hand you can call the company once again and enroll in their DRIP program. The phone representative, or a brochure they send you, will tell you all you need to know. You will need your stock certificate number to enroll.
5. Once you have enrolled, store the stock certificate in a secure place like a safe deposit box. Hopefully it will stay there for many decades while your dividends, regular new investments, and capital gains grow into a small fortune.

APPENDIX 3
RECOMMENDED INDEX MUTUAL FUNDS

As I noted in Chapter 5, I do not recommend mutual funds as a general rule. However on pages 83-84 I mentioned that index funds are an exception to the rule and are worthwhile to own. Read the information on those pages, and if you are interested, here are the phone numbers for further information.

1. TIAA (Teachers Insurance and Annuity Association)
   The highest quality and lowest priced insurance and annuity products available in America. Only school employees or hospital employees are eligible. Day school, Yeshivah, and Beis Yaakov employees should check if they are eligible for these products.
   The Teacher's Personal Annuity (TPA) Stock Index Fund

or the College Retirement Equities Fund (CREF) Stock Fund are excellent funds with very low expenses. The latter fund is not a pure index fund but it has earned about 15 percent annually for 40 years with the lowest expenses in the industry. As a medical instructor with my own private pension plan I was only eligible for the TPA Stock Index Fund, but I would have bought the CREF Stock Fund as well if I was allowed.

- 1-800-223-1200 Monday through Friday 8 A.M. to 8 P.M. Eastern Time

For questions about the Teachers Personal Annuity, including the Stock Index Account, as well as insurance questions

- 1-800-842-2776 Monday through Friday 8 A.M. to 11 P.M. Eastern Time.

To speak with a consultant about retirement savings and planning as well as annuity options

2. Vanguard Index 500 Fund

An excellent fund with very low expenses which tracks the Standard & Poors 500 with a buy-and-hold strategy. Over the last 20 years it has returned about 15 percent annually.

- 1-800-662-7447 General information and prospectuses

- 1-800-662-2003 Information on retirement plans (other than IRA's)

- 1-800-662-2739 Information on IRA's

APPENDIX 4

SAMPLE INVESTMENT PROGRAMS

On the following pages, several investments programs are outlined. Sample results are shown for investing for retirement at age 60 or to pay for a child's wedding and/or *kollel* when they are 20.

Varying annualized rates of return are illustrated. Assume that banks will pay about 2 percent, bonds 5 percent, and stocks over the long-term 10 percent. Coca-Cola has grown at an annual average of about 15 percent, so that is shown as well.

Several fundamental facts are well demonstrated:

1. The earlier you start, the far greater amount you will accumulate, no matter what the annual yield.

2. You will achieve far greater long-term success if you choose stocks over banks or bonds.

3. Even small amounts like $100 to start and $10 weekly can add up to millions if invested steadily and patiently over decades.

The yields illustrated assume the reinvestment of all dividends and interest. Taxes have not been taken into consideration. Generally, if the investments are held for a child, taxes may be minimized; if the investments are in a pension account, taxes are irrelevant until the pension is drawn upon. Please consult with your tax adviser.

PROGRAM 1
$100 to start and $10 added per week until age 60

STARTING AGE	ANNUAL INVESTMENT RETURN			
	2%	5%	10%	15%
Newborn	60,635	200,195	2,120,688	10,000,000+
Bar mitzvah 13	40,803	99,574	574,895	4,066,876
20	32,077	67,110	283,060	1,423,054
30	21,551	36,623	100,947	315,521
40	12,933	18,128	33,886	133,726
50	5,877	6,907	9,193	12,483
amount shown is value, in dollars, at age 60				

PROGRAM 2
$2,000 to start and $40 per week (amounts allowable in IRA) until age 60

STARTING AGE	ANNUAL INVESTMENT RETURN			
	2%	5%	10%	15%
Newborn	247,851	832,868	9,124,530	10,000,000+
Bar mitzvah 13	167,308	415,054	2,474,706	10,000,000+
20	131,871	280,253	1,219,265	6,332,154
30	89,122	153,660	435,832	1,405,182
40	54,121	76,860	147,347	303,450
50	25,463	30,266	41,117	57,089
amount shown is value, in dollars, at age 60				

PROGRAM 3
Investing for newborn to age 20 for a wedding and/or *kollel*

$100 to start and $10 per week for newborn to age 20		$2000 to start and $40 per week for newborn to age 20	
Annual Return	Amount Accumulated	Annual Return	Amount Accumulated
2%	12,933	2%	54,121
5%	18,128	5%	76,860
10%	33,886	10%	147,347
15%	67,863	15%	303,450
amount shown is value, in dollars, at age 20			

APPENDIX 5

CUSTOMIZING THE PLAN

Suggestions on purchasing the stocks which I have described in this book

There are various approaches which one might take if one decides to follow the advice in this book and buy stocks for the long term with reinvested dividends. I will give some suggestions below.

Obviously each individual circumstance is unique and the reader may have to consult a professional, such as an accountant or financial planner, for specific advice relevant to each person's situation. However, be aware that most professionals have personal agendas, such as selling you something so they can earn a commission, which could cloud their judgment and present potential conflicts of interest. That is why I make most of my investing decisions on my own, utilize a discount broker frequently, and believe in a hands-off long-term approach with little buying and selling. Be aware that professionals you speak to may disparage my approach in order to guide you toward a financial product which they want to sell you. They lose money if you buy stocks directly from a company and reinvest dividends at no cost. So be careful concerning any financial advice you receive from professionals such as accountants, brokers, insurance agents, or lawyers.

If a person has the time and interest to research companies on their own, that is fine. I wish you all the best. You may find the advice given in Chapter 9 of this book very helpful as a guide on how to analyze individual companies. The advice below is specifically geared for someone who would simply like to buy the stocks which I have bought and sink or swim with me. I cannot absolutely promise never to sell any of my stocks. For the most part however, I buy and hold for the long term and will more or less keep the stocks I mention in this book for many years to come. I have put my money where my mouth is.

I believe that adequate warnings about the risks of the stock market have already been expressed in the body of this book. Before I give the specific advice below, let me repeat some of these warnings:

1. Do not buy and sell regularly. Buy and hold for the long term.

2. Reinvest all dividends.

3. Never, ever, ever buy stocks with money you may need in five years or less. Be extremely cautious about buying stocks with money needed in less than 10 years. With a time frame of 10 years or more, quality stocks can be a safe investment. With longer time frames of 20, 30, or 40 years, the risks drop dramatically. Warren Buffett has said, "Do not own a stock for 10 seconds unless you plan to hold it for at least 10 years."

4. Do not panic and sell when stocks go down. That is often a time to buy more quality stocks on sale. Warren Buffett has said, "Do not own stocks unless you can stand to see the value of your investment go down at times by 50 percent."

5. Diversify adequately among companies and industries.

For the appropriately forewarned, here is some specific investing advice.

1. THE PERSON WITH $22,000 OR MORE TO INVEST

A simple approach would be to buy equal dollar amounts of each of my stocks and reinvest the dividends. I more or less purchased equal dollar amounts of each of my stocks over the years. I don't recommend doing this unless you can purchase at least $1000 of each stock or the commissions will be prohibitively high. There are minimum commission levels and on small purchases the commission is too large a percentage of the purchase price to be economical.

2. THE PERSON WHO WANTS TO PUT $1000 IN EACH STOCK BUT DOESN'T HAVE ENOUGH MONEY TO BUY ALL 22

This of course requires picking from the 22. For example, a person with $10,000 to invest may want to buy 10 stocks, a person with $8000 may want to buy 8 stocks, etc. I am reluctant to pick and chose among my 22. It was hard enough narrowing down 1700 stocks to my 22 and therefore it is difficult to narrow down any further. But if I was forced to chose a few, here is what I would probably recommend.

If I could only buy one stock, it would probably be Coca-Cola. I simply love this stock. A single share purchased for $42 when the company went public in 1919 would be worth $500,000 today without reinvested dividends. With reinvested dividends that single share would today be worth over $5 million. The company sells soda in over 80 countries and the product is well protected against any local recessions. The stock is virtually an international mutual fund all by itself. The company sells a simple product with universal appeal. The marketing is second to none. Not very much research and development is required. You can predict that 50 years from now the company will pretty much be doing the same thing it does today. Thirst will always be thirst. The company steadily and consistently raises the dividend.

If I had to pick some others I suppose they would be the following:

1. **UTILITIES** — Duke Energy or Tampa Electric for electric utility. Cincinnati Bell or American Water Works for other utilities.

2. **BANKS** — Either PNC or Wachovia is an excellent bank stock.

3. **CONSUMER PRODUCTS** — Coca-Cola first, then Gillette second.

4. **PHARMACEUTICALS** — All four are excellent but I would probably pick in descending order Merck, Bristol-Myers Squibb, Abbott Labs, Eli Lilly.

5. **INDUSTRY AND TECHNOLOGY** — General Electric and Hewlett Packard first, with either Boeing or 3M or Dover Corp. as a third pick.

6. **NO-DIVIDEND OR LOW-DIVIDEND PAYING HIGH-TECH** — If you want a little excitement, then either Microsoft or Intel is excellent. Intel does pay a small and rapidly rising dividend so you may want to buy it first.

3. A PERSON WHO HAS SMALLER AMOUNTS TO INVEST

As I just noted above, if you have to buy only one stock, make it Coca-Cola. Buy a single share or more from a broker, and then buy additional amounts commission free directly from the company for as little as $10 at a shot. Do this for many years and you may turn out to be very wealthy. As you get more capital to invest you can pick additional stocks from the ones I mention above. Diversification is important so each time you add a stock, pick from a different category.

My oldest son Elchonan owns three stocks, Coca-Cola, Hershey, and Johnson and Johnson. He faithfully adds between $10 and $50 every month or so (he saves $3 per week from his allowance and also invests birthday money from Bubby and Zeidy).

4. A PERSON WHO HAS SMALLER AMOUNTS TO INVEST AND WANTS TO AVOID INDIVIDUAL STOCKS

The two index mutual funds mentioned in Appendix 3 are both excellent and I own both. They give you instant diversification with minimal time, effort, and risk. I add $100 per month to each. My younger boys Moshe Eliezer and Chaim Mordechai save $3 per week and when they have $50 saved they send it to the Vanguard Index 500 Fund. They also invest birthday money from Bubby and Zeidy. My girls Shoshana Miriam and Shira Malka are still babies so my wife and I invest birthday money from Bubby and Zeidy as well as some added money from ourselves into the Vanguard Index 500 Fund on their behalf.

See Appendix 3 for minimal amounts to start and to add to these mutual funds.

APPENDIX 6

PLEASE, TAKE NOTE

How to remember and access your learning

"The inhabitants of Judea, who were precise in their language and kept notes, retained their Torah"

(Eiruvin 53a)

Several years ago, *The Jewish Observer* presented a series of articles concerning the importance of learning large quantities of Talmud (*bekiyus*) and described several programs with that goal in mind. The need for learning *bekiyus* as one of the prerequisites for being a *talmid chacham* was stated eloquently and need not be repeated here. A layman with family and financial burdens, or someone with many activities in *klal* work, may feel that he cannot reap the rewards of learning large amounts of Talmud for *bekiyus* because it is obvious that constant review is necessary for any of these programs to succeed. A busy layman may have enough time to learn a *daf* a day or a *perek* of *Mishnah* a day, but he may not have enough time to review his studies more than once, if at all, if he is to keep a steady pace going, as in *Daf Yomi.*

This appendix originally appeared in *The Jewish Observer,* March 1985.

I myself was confronted with this situation. I am a medical doctor who is a *baal teshuvah*. I became observant in medical school, and therefore had a need to cover large areas of material quickly, as I had a lot of catching up to do. I did take three years off from medicine to attend yeshivos, but this was not enough. So now I must learn intensely while in the middle of residency training, a very busy time by anyone's standards. Although I recently finished the first half of *Shas Bavli* (the complete Babylonian Talmud), and am working on my fourth *siyum* of the entire *Mishnah*, my main problem is finding time for adequate review.

It was to this end that my wife, while she was still my *kallah*, suggested that I keep notes summarizing my daily learning. Taking notes can serve two basic functions. Firstly, in order to put down in writing the material he has learned, a person must first organize his knowledge in an understandable and concise way. Secondly, the notes can serve as an extremely powerful index and reference source, thereby aiding someone who does not have the kind of time necessary for a proper review that leads to full retention of numerous facts.

STARTING WITH "MISHNAYOS"

For my *Mishnayos* learning, I summarized each *perek, mishnah* by *mishnah*, in English and/or Hebrew. Whenever I saw the same topic repeated in another *Mishnah*, I would indicate the source of the new *Mishnah* next to the original entry and vice versa. For example, "*hamotzi mamon machaveiro alov hareiyah*" (the burden of proof lies on the person wanting to extract money) comes up numerous times in *Mishnayos*. I put all the places it comes up in parentheses next to the appropriate summarized *Mishnayos* that discuss the idea. So, as long as I can remember one place where this idea presents itself, I have automatic access to all the other sources. Likewise for *bereirah*,[1] *peh she'asur peh she'hitter*[2] and innumerable other

---

1. A type of selection that takes effect retroactively, which has application in circumstances throughout *Shas*.

2. Limited liability in case of confessional evidence — a rule in jurisprudence (*Nezikin*).

topics widespread through *Shas Mishnayos*. The reference systems found in the standard editions of *Shas Bavli* and *Shas Mishnayos* only cross refer to another place that has the exact same words. My notes are thematic, and cross-refer to any other *Mishnah* that discusses the same idea or a relevant idea, even if the wording is different.

In addition, I summarized the main ideas of an entire *Mesechta* (tractate) and filed it at the beginning of the *Mishnah*-by-*Mishnah* summaries of that *Mesechta*. For example, there are ten factors that can invalidate a *get* (a divorce document) by Torah law. At the beginning of my summaries of the *Mishnayos* for *Gittin*, I listed all 10 factors and listed next to each the *Mishnayos* in which it could be found. Should I want to review the idea of *k'sivah lishmo* (intent at time of writing a *get*), for instance, all I need do is look at my list and I am immediately referred to numerous *Mishnayos* discussing this idea. Likewise, there are five things that invalidate *shechitah* (ritual slaughter) by Torah law. I summarized the five things at the beginning of *Mesechta Chullin*. So if I want to look up the idea of *derisah* or *shehiyah*, for example, I immediately know which *Mishnayos* to look in.

NO REPLACEMENT FOR REVIEW

This does not replace the need for review — and I would never even suggest that, as *Chazal* have repeatedly stressed, the need for review. But it does help someone who wants to learn *bekiyus* but cannot *presently* review sufficiently to retain his learning. As long as I can remember one place where a widespread idea was discussed, I have all the other references automatically at my fingertips.

If I want to review a major idea of *Gittin, Chullin,* etc. all I need do is look at my notes for that *Mesechta* and my indices will direct me to whichever *Mishnayos* I should consult. Similarly, if I know that a certain idea is mentioned somewhere in a certain *seder,* in a matter of minutes I can run through my English notes until I find the appropriate reference. It is certainly easier and quicker to review a few pages of English notes than to review the actual text of numerous *Mesechtas* until I find the appropriate reference!

ENHANCING MY GEMARA

These notes also greatly enhance my *Gemara* learning. For example, I was recently learning a *Tosafos* in *Kiddushin* and I knew that a *Mishnah* that I had learned somewhere in *Temurah* would have been most helpful. Nowhere in the *Tosafos* was a reference to *Temurah* even made. Using my notes, I found the needed *Mishnah* and was able to understand the *Tosafos* much better. This type of thing happens, if not daily, then almost so. Literally hundreds of times my *Mishnah* notes have helped me to locate facts spread out in the entire six *sedarim* of *Mishnayos*, to help me to understand a *Gemara* or *Tosafos*.

I also keep a similar set of notes on *Shas Bavli*. I make a brief (one-to-three line) summary of each *sugya* in English and/or Hebrew. I also cross-refer, as in my *Mishnayos* notes. I keep a separate loose-leaf book for each *seder*. So far I have complete summaries of all *Bavli* from *Zeraim, Moed* and *Nashim*. So, if I know that I learned a certain *Gemara* somewhere in the second half of *Kiddushin,* for example, that will help me in *Yevamos,* it takes a matter of minutes using my notes to find where the needed *Gemara* comes in. Then I can review the desired *Gemara* from the text. The point is that looking through a few pages of English notes is a lot quicker than searching the last 50 pages of *Kiddushin* on the inside, looking for the needed *Gemara*.

Therefore, someone who cannot presently review his learning from the text can use *Mishnah* and *Gemara* notes of his own style, in his own handwriting, to aid his memory and to prevent himself from losing what he has gained. I knew that the quote that started off this article was somewhere in *Mesechta Eiruvin* between *daf* 50 and *daf* 70. To have reviewed 20 pages of *Gemara* on the inside to find the needed quote would have taken a long time, and perhaps discouraged me from writing this article. Using my notes, I was able to locate the needed quote in a matter of minutes.

Below is a sample of my notes for the beginning of *Mishnayos Gittin*. The items on the right-hand margin are the 10 factors that invalidate a *get* by Torah law. Listed next to each item is the *perek* and *Mishnah* that discuss the *inyan*. After these 10 items is a summary of the first chapter. The items in parentheses refer to pertinent cross references that discuss the same or a relevant idea. The notes summarizing each chapter read from left to right as I use English syntax with Hebrew words inserted.

10 REQUIREMENTS FOR A כשר GET

גיטין

1) לרצונו – פרק ט, משנה ח

2) בכתב – פרק ב, משנה ג; פרק ט, משנה ג

3) לשמו ולשמה – פרק א, משנה א; פרק ב, משנה ה; פרק ג, משנה א,ב; פרק ד, משנה ב; פרק ח, משנה ה

4) כורת לגמרי – פרק ט, משנה א,ב

5) הוא נותן – פרק ד, משנה א; פרק ו, משנה א; פרק ח, משנה ב

6) היא מקבלת – פרק ד, משנה א; פרק ו, משנה א; פרק ח, משנה א

7) היא נשלחת –פרק ח, משנה ב

8) בעדים – פרק א, משנה א; פרק ב, משנה ד,ה; פרק ד משנה ג; פרק ו, משנה ב; פרק ט, משנה ד,ו,ז

9) וכתב ונתן – פרק ב, משנה ג,ד; פרק ט, משנה ד

10) בתורת גט – פרק ח, משנה ב

נשים - פרק א

1) Bringing a גט from מדינת הים — requirement to say בפני נכתב
ובפני נחתם — (משנה א).

2) What are boundaries of ארץ ישראל for גיטין? (משנה ב).

3) Bringing a גט in ארץ ישראל itself — must you still say בפני
נכתב ? (משנה ג) וכו'.

4) What if you can't say בפני נכתב ובפני נחתם? (משנה ג). (Also
see ו פרק ב, משנה).

5) Comparison of גיטי נשים to שחרורי עבדים (משנה ד-ו). (Also
see מס' קדושין, פרק א משנה ג).